Hana's Suitcase on Stage

Original story by
Karen Levine

Play by
Emil Sher

Second
Story
Press

Library and Archives Canada Cataloguing in Publication

Levine, Karen, 1955-
Sher, Emil, 1959-
Hana's suitcase on stage : play / by Emil Sher ; original story by Karen Levine.

(The Holocaust remembrance series for young readers)
Includes text of play and original story by Karen Levine on which the play is based.
ISBN 978-1-897187-05-0

1. Brady, Hana—Juvenile drama. 2. Brady, Hana—Juvenile literature.
3. Jewish children in the Holocaust—Czech Republic—Nové Mesto nad
Metují—Juvenile drama. 4. Jewish children in the Holocaust—Czech
Republic—Nové Mesto nad Metují—Biography—Juvenile literature.
5. Holocaust, Jewish (1939-1945)—Czech Republic—Nové Mesto nad
Metují—Juvenile drama. 6. Holocaust, Jewish (1939-1945)—Czech
Republic—Nové Mesto nad Metují—Biography—Juvenile literature.
7. Theresienstadt (Concentration camp)—Juvenile drama. 8. Theresienstadt
(Concentration camp)—Juvenile literature. 9. Holocaust, Jewish
(1939-1945)—Study and teaching—Japan—Juvenile drama. 10. Holocaust,
Jewish (1939-1945)—Study and teaching—Japan—Juvenile literature. I. Levine,
Karen, 1955- Hana's suitcase. II. Title. III. Series: Holocaust remembrance book for young readers.

PS8587.H38535H35 2006   jC812'.54   C2006-900075-1

Editor: Margie Wolfe
Design: Stephanie Martin and Lancaster Reid Creative

Front cover photo: *Hana's Suitcase* at Lorraine Kimsa Theatre for Young People (Mar. 4-Apr. 23/06)
Jessica Greenberg (Hana); Photo by Daniel Alexander.

Document on page 61 from the Terezin Ghetto Museum. Reprinted with permission.

Second Story Press gratefully acknowledges the support of the Ontario Arts Council and the Canada Council for the Arts for our publishing program. We acknowledge the financial support of the Government of Canada through the Book Publishing Industry Development Program.

Canada Council
for the Arts

Conseil des Arts
du Canada

Published by
SECOND STORY PRESS
20 Maud Street, Suite 401
Toronto, ON
M5V 2M5

www.secondstorypress.ca

Hana's Suitcase on Stage

Second Story Press would like to thank George Brady and his family for generously allowing us to use his family photographs and documents in this book. We would also like to express our appreciation to Fumiko Ishioka and the Holocaust Education Resource Center in Tokyo for sharing their photographs and materials here as well. We are grateful to Ludmilla Chládková from the Terezin Ghetto Museum (which rarely closes) for her on-going support.

Hana's Suitcase

by
Karen Levine

A TRUE STORY

For my parents,
Helen and Gil Levine.

Introduction

Hana's Suitcase is a true story that takes place on three continents over a period of almost seventy years. It brings together the experiences of a girl and her family in Czechoslovakia in the 1930s and 40s, a young woman and a group of children in Tokyo, Japan, and a man in Toronto, Canada in modern times.

Between 1939 and 1945, the world was at war. Nazi dictator Adolf Hitler wanted Germany to rule the globe. At the center of his vision was the brutal elimination of the Jewish people from the face of the earth. To get rid of his "enemies," he set up dozens of prison camps — called concentration camps — across Europe. Jewish women, men and children from almost every country on the continent were deported; they were torn from their homes and sent to the camps, where they endured terrible suffering. Many people died of hunger and disease. Most were murdered. In these death camps and elsewhere — where Hitler's followers carried out his terrible plan — six million Jews were killed. One-and-a-half million Jewish children were among them.

In 1945, the war ended and the entire world learned the horrors of what had gone on in the concentration camps. Since then, people have been trying to understand more about what is today known as the "Holocaust," the worst example of mass murder — or genocide — in human history. How did it happen? How can we make sure it will never happen again?

In Japan, a country allied with Nazi Germany during the Second World War, attention to the history of the Holocaust is relatively new. An anonymous Japanese donor, who wanted to contribute to global tolerance and understanding, decided it was important for young people in Japan to learn more about this aspect of world history. Single-handedly, this donor has endowed the Tokyo Holocaust Education Resource Center, which is dedicated to that purpose.

At a Children's Forum on the Holocaust held in 1999, two hundred students from schools in the Tokyo area met Holocaust survivor Yaffa Eliach. She told them about how almost every Jew in her village, young and old, was murdered by the Nazis. At the end of her talk, she reminded her audience that children have the power "to create peace in the future." A dozen of the young Japanese people there took her challenge to heart and formed a group called "Small Wings." Now the members of Small Wings, aged eight to eighteen, meet every month. They publish a newsletter, help run the Tokyo Holocaust Education Resource Center and work to interest other Japanese children in the history of the Holocaust. They do their work under the guidance of Fumiko Ishioka, the director of the Tokyo Holocaust Center.

The suitcase — Hana's suitcase — is a key to the success of their mission. In it lies a story of terrible sadness and great joy, a reminder of the brutality of the past and of hope for the future.

Tokyo, Japan, Winter 2000

REALLY, IT'S A VERY ORDINARY LOOKING SUITCASE. A little tattered around the edges, but in good condition.

It's brown. It's big. You could fit quite a lot in it — clothes for a long trip, maybe. Books, games, treasures, toys. But there is nothing inside it now.

Every day children come to a little museum in Tokyo, Japan to see this suitcase. It sits in a glass cabinet. And through the glass you can see that there is writing on the suitcase. In white paint, across the front, there is a girl's name: Hana Brady. A date of birth: May 16, 1931. And one other word: *Waisenkind*. That's the German word for orphan.

The Japanese children know that the suitcase came from Auschwitz, a concentration camp where millions of people suffered and died during the Second World War between 1939 and 1945. But who was Hana Brady? Where did she come from? Where was she travelling to? What did she pack? How did she become an orphan? What kind of girl was she and what happened to her?

The children are full of questions. So is the director of the museum, a slender young woman with long black hair named Fumiko Ishioka.

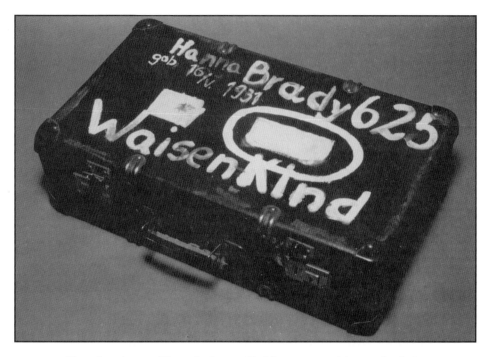

Hana's suitcase. Though she spelled her name with one "n," the German spelling has two, as on the suitcase.

Fumiko and the children gently take the suitcase out of the glass case and open it. They search the side pockets. Maybe Hana left something that would be a clue. Nothing. They look under the polka-dot lining. There are no hints there either.

Fumiko promises the children to do everything she can to find out about the girl who owned the suitcase, to solve the mystery. And for the next year, she becomes a detective, scouring the world for clues to the story of Hana Brady.

Nové Město na Moravě, Czechoslovakia, 1930s

IN ROLLING HILLS in the middle of what was then Czechoslovakia, in a province called Moravia, there was a town called Nové Město na Moravě. It wasn't big, but it was famous. And in the winter, especially, it was a very busy place. People from all over the country came to cross-country ski in Nové Město na Moravě. There were races to be raced. There were trails to be blazed and there were frozen ponds for skating. In the summer, there was swimming, sailing, fishing and camping.

Nové Město na Moravě was home to 4,000 people. Once the town was well known for making glass. But in the 1930s, people worked in the forests and in little workshops that made skis. On the main street, there was a large, two-story white building. It had a two-story attic. And in its basement, a secret passageway led to a church on the town's main square. In olden days, when the town was under siege, it was used by soldiers to store food and supplies for the people of Nové Město na Moravě.

The town's general store was on the ground floor. There, you could buy almost anything — buttons, jam, oil lamps and rakes, sleigh bells, stones for sharpening knives, dishes, paper and pens and candy. On the second floor lived the Brady family: father Karel, mother Marketa, Hana and her big brother George.

The town of Nové Město na Moravě and its surroundings.

Father worked six days a week in the store. He was an athlete, known to almost everyone in Nové Město na Moravě for his love of soccer, skiing and gymnastics. He was also an amateur actor with a big booming voice that could be heard from one end of a playing field to the other. Because of this, Father was chosen to call the cross-country ski races over a megaphone, so that everyone could hear the action. He was a volunteer firefighter who, with other men from the town, rode the fire engine to help people in emergencies.

The Brady family opened their home to artists of all kinds — musicians, painters and poets, sculptors and actors. When they were hungry, they could always find a hot meal, produced by Boshka, the family housekeeper and cook. And their artistic talents found an eager audience, which, of course, included two impish children — Hana and George. Sometimes George was called upon to play his violin. Hana was more than willing to demonstrate her skill on the piano to anyone who would listen. And in the middle of the living room, there was a record player that was cranked up by hand. Hana played her favorite song — "I Have Nine Canaries" — over and over again.

Hana in costume for a school play.

Mother was a warm and generous hostess with a good sense of humor and a very loud laugh. She, too, worked six days a week in the store and people often came in just to hear her jokes and banter. She paid special attention to poor people in Nové Město na Moravě who lived on the outskirts of town. Once a week, she would prepare a bundle of food and clothing that Hana would deliver to needy neighbors. Hana was very proud of her mission and she nagged her mother to make care packages more often.

Hana was a helper in the store, too. From the time they were very small, Hana and George had the job of keeping the shelves stocked, clean and tidy. They learned how to slice yeast, chisel small lumps off the sugar loaf, weigh spices and seasonings, and

Nové Město na Moravě. The Brady family lived on the second floor of the fourth building from the left. Their store was on the main floor.

twist paper into the shape of hollow cones to be filled with candy and sold as treats. Once in a while, Mother noticed that some of those candy cones were missing. Hana never told on George. And he never told on Hana.

There were always cats around the store, who worked full-time as mouse catchers. But once, as a special treat, Mother and Father ordered fluffy white angora kittens as pets for the children. Two soft little bundles arrived through the mail in a box with breathing holes. At first, Sylva, the family wolfhound, a huge grey furry creature, sniffed around them suspiciously. But soon the kittens, who Hana named Micki and Mourek, became accepted members of the family.

Hana and George went to the public school. They were average kids, who got into regular mischief and had the usual problems and triumphs. There was just one thing that was different about them.

The Bradys were Jewish. They weren't a religious family. But Mother and Father wanted the children to know about their heritage. Once a week, while their playmates were at church, Hana and George sat with a special teacher who taught them about Jewish holidays and Jewish history.

There were a few other Jewish families in Nové Město na Moravě. But Hana and George were the only Jewish children in the town. In their early years no one really noticed or cared that they were different. Soon, though, the fact that they were Jews would become the most important thing about them.

Tokyo,
Winter 2000

BACK IN HER OFFICE, half a world away in Japan and more than half a century later, Fumiko Ishioka remembered how the suitcase had come to her.

In 1998, she had begun her job as coordinator of a small museum, called the Tokyo Holocaust Center. It was dedicated to teaching Japanese children about the Holocaust. At a conference in Israel, Fumiko had met a few Holocaust survivors, people who had lived through the horrors of the concentration camps. She was

The Holocaust Education Resource Center in Tokyo, Japan.

Fumiko teaching children at the Center about the Holocaust.

astonished by their optimism and their joy in living, despite everything they had been through. When Fumiko felt sad about things in her own life, she often thought about these survivors. They were so strong-willed and wise. They had so much to teach her.

Fumiko wanted young people in Japan to learn from the Holocaust as well. It was her job to make it happen. And it wasn't an easy one. How, she wondered, could she help Japanese children understand the terrible story of what happened to millions of Jewish children on a faraway continent over fifty years ago?

She decided the best way to start would be through physical objects that the children could see and touch. She wrote to Jewish and Holocaust museums all over the world — in Poland, Germany, the United States and Israel — asking for a loan of artifacts that had belonged to children. She posted her request on the Internet. She wrote to individuals she thought might be able to help. Fumiko was looking for a pair of shoes and for a suitcase.

Fumiko Ishioka and one of the children visiting the Center.

Everyone turned her down, telling her that the objects they had so carefully preserved were too precious to send to such a small museum, so far away. Fumiko wasn't sure what to do next. But she wasn't the kind of person who gave up easily. Just the opposite. The more rejections she got, the more dedicated she became.

That fall, Fumiko travelled to Poland where many Nazi concentration camps had been located. There, on the site of the most well-known camp, she visited the Auschwitz Museum. Fumiko begged for a short meeting with the Museum's assistant director. She was given five minutes to explain what she wanted. When she left the assistant director's office, she had a promise that her request would be considered.

A few months later, a package from the Auschwitz Museum arrived: a child's sock and shoe, a child's sweater, a can of Zyklon B poisonous gas and one suitcase — Hana's suitcase.

Nové Město na Moravě, 1938

HANA HAD BLONDE HAIR, blue eyes and a very pretty round face. She was a strong girl. Once in a while, Hana would provoke a battle with George, just to show off her muscles. Even though her brother was three years older, Hana would sometimes emerge the winner. But most of the time, Hana and George played well together.

In the summer, in the creek behind their house, they pretended to be in the navy. Climbing into an old wooden washtub, the children sailed along until one or the other pulled the plug in the middle and they sank, laughing and splashing. There were three different kinds of swings in the backyard meadow — one for a small child, a two-seater, and one that swung from a giant tree out over the creek. Sometimes, the neighborhood children would gather there for swinging contests. Who could swing the highest? Who could jump the farthest? Often it was Hana.

In the long halls of their apartment over the store, Hana raced on her red scooter, George on his blue one. In the winter, Hana and George built snow forts and skied. But Hana's greatest love was skating, and she worked hard perfecting her pirouettes on Nové Město na Moravě's frozen pond. Sometimes, when she wore her special red skating outfit — the one with the white fur on the ends of the sleeves — she imagined herself a dancing princess. Her

Hana loved to play outdoors when she was young.

parents, her friends and her brother applauded both the performance and the dream.

Because her parents worked six days a week, Sunday mornings were special for the family. When they woke up, George and Hana would snuggle up in their parents' bed under the fluffy feather comforter. On Sunday afternoons in the summer, they would all pile into the car and head off to the nearest fort or castle for a picnic, sometimes with Uncle Ludvik and Aunt Hedda who also lived in Nové Město na Moravě. In the winter, there were sleigh rides and long cross-country skiing adventures. Hana was a very strong skier. On the eight-kilometer run between Nové Město na Moravě and a nearby village (which had a wonderful tearoom with delicious creamy pastries), Hana always led the big family pack of cousins, even though she was the youngest.

But by New Year's Eve 1938, there was a new and menacing feeling in the air. There was talk of war. Adolf Hitler and his Nazis were in power in Germany. Earlier that year, Hitler had taken over Austria. Then he had marched his armies into parts of Czechoslovakia. Refugees — people trying to escape the Nazis — started appearing at the Bradys' door, asking for money, food and shelter. They always found a warm welcome from Mother and Father. But the children were mystified. Who are these people? Hana wondered. Why are they coming here? Why don't they want to stay in their own homes?

In the evenings, after Hana and George had been sent to bed, Mother and Father would sit by the radio and listen to the news. Often friends came and joined them, and they would talk long into the night about the news they had heard. "We'll keep our voices down," they would say, "so as not to wake the children."

The conversation of the adults was so intense, the discussions so heated, that they rarely heard the squeak

Hana in her special red skating outfit.

of floorboards in the darkened hall, as Hana and George tiptoed to their secret listening post just outside the living room. The children heard the talk about the new anti-Jewish laws in Austria. They heard about *Kristallnacht* in Germany, when gangs of Nazi thugs roamed through Jewish neighborhoods, breaking windows in homes and stores, burning synagogues, and beating people in the streets.

"It couldn't happen here, could it?" Hana whispered to her brother.

"Shhhh," said George. "If we talk now, they'll hear us and we'll be sent back to bed."

One night, their neighbor Mr. Rott presented a shocking idea to the adults. "We can all feel that a war is coming," he began.

Both Hana and George learned to ski when they were very young.

"It's not safe for Jews to be here. We should all leave Nové Město na Moravě, leave Czechoslovakia, for America, for Palestine, for Canada. For anywhere. Leave now, before it's too late."

The rest of the group was taken aback. "Are you crazy, Mr. Rott?" one asked. "This is our home. This is where we belong." And that settled that.

Despite the bad times, the Bradys were determined to celebrate the coming of 1939. On New Year's Eve, after a feast of turkey, sausage, salami and pudding, the children got ready to play the traditional game of predicting the future. Hana, George, and their young cousins from nearby towns were given half a walnut into which they each wedged a small candle. A large basin of water was dragged into the middle of the room. Each child launched a little walnut boat into it. Eleven-year-old George's boat wobbled in the water, turned round and round, and finally came to a stop, lopsided. His candle kept burning. Eight-year-old Hana launched hers and, for a moment, it glided along without a quiver. Then it shook, turned on its side, and the candle hit the water and went out.

Tokyo,
March 2000

FROM THE DAY THE SUITCASE arrived in Tokyo, Fumiko and the children were drawn to it. Ten-year-old Akira, who usually loved to joke and tease, wondered aloud what it would be like to be an orphan. Maiko, who was older, loved to party and was an accomplished synchronized swimmer. She always became very quiet in the presence of the suitcase. It made her think about being sent away from her own friends.

The suitcase was the only object they had at the Center that was linked to a name. From the date on the suitcase, Fumiko and the children figured out that Hana would have been thirteen years old when she was sent to Auschwitz. A year younger than me, said one girl. Just as old as my big sister, said Akira.

Fumiko wrote back to the Auschwitz Museum. Could they help her find out anything about the girl who owned the suitcase? No, they replied. They knew no more than she did. Fumiko reported back to the children. "Try somewhere else," Maiko urged. "Don't give up," said Akira. The kids chanted encouragement like a chorus: "Keep on looking." Fumiko promised to do just that.

Fumiko wrote to Yad Vashem, Israel's Holocaust museum. No, we have never heard of a girl named Hana Brady, the director wrote. Have you tried the Holocaust Memorial Museum in Washington, DC? Fumiko rushed a letter off to Washington, but the reply was the same. We have no information about a girl named Hana Brady. How discouraging it was!

Then, out of the blue, Fumiko received a note from the museum at Auschwitz. They had discovered something. They had found Hana's name on a list. It showed that Hana had come to Auschwitz from a place called Theresienstadt.

Nové Město na Moravě, 1939

On March 15, 1939, Hitler's Nazi troops marched into the rest of Czechoslovakia and the Brady family's life was changed forever. The Nazis declared that Jews were evil, a bad influence, dangerous. From now on, the Brady family and the other Jews in Nové Město na Moravě would have to live by different rules.

Jews could only leave their houses at certain hours of the day. They could only shop in certain stores and only at certain times. Jews weren't allowed to travel, so there were no more visits to beloved aunts, uncles, and grandmothers in nearby towns. The Bradys were forced to tell the Nazis about everything they owned — art, jewellery, cutlery, bank books. They hurriedly stashed their most precious papers under the shingles in the attic. Father's stamp collection and Mother's silver were hidden with Gentile, non-Jewish friends. But the family radio had to be taken to a central office and surrendered to a Nazi official.

One day, Hana and George lined up at the movie theater to see "Snow White and the Seven Dwarfs." When they got to the ticket box they saw a sign that read "No Jews Allowed." Their faces red, their eyes burning, Hana and George turned on their heels and headed for home. When Hana walked in the door, she was furious and very upset. "What is happening to us? Why can't I go

Hana and George stood by each other as the Nazi restrictions increased.

to the movies? Why can't I just ignore the sign?" Mother and Father looked grimly at each other. There were no easy answers.

Every week seemed to bring a new restriction. No Jews in the playground. No Jews on the sports fields. No Jews in the parks. Soon Hana could no longer go to the gym. Even the skating pond was declared off limits. Her friends — all of them Gentiles — at first were as mystified by the rules as Hana. They sat together in school as they always had, and still had good times making mischief in the classroom and in private backyards. "We'll be together forever, no matter what," promised Hana's best friend Maria. "We're not going to let anyone tell us who we can play with!"

But gradually, as the months dragged on, all Hana's playmates, even Maria, stopped coming over after school and on the weekends. Maria's parents had ordered her to stay away from Hana. They were afraid the Nazis would punish their whole family for allowing Maria to be friends with a Jewish child. Hana was terribly lonely.

With each loss of friendship and with each new restriction, Hana and George felt their world grow a little smaller. They were angry. They were sad. And they were frustrated. "What can we do?" they asked their parents. "Where can we go now?"

Mother and Father tried their best to distract the children, to help them find new ways to have fun. "We are lucky," Mother told them, "because we have such a big garden. You can play hide-and-seek. You can swing from the trees. You can invent games. You can play detective in the storerooms. You can explore the secret tunnel. You can play charades. Be grateful that you have each other!"

Hana and George were grateful to have each other and they did play together, but it didn't make them feel any better about all the things they couldn't do anymore, all the places they couldn't go. On a fine spring day, when the sun was shining, the two of them sat in the meadow, bored, fiddling with the grass. Suddenly Hana burst into tears. "It's not fair," she cried. "I hate this. I want it to be like it was before." She yanked a fistful of grass out of the ground and threw it in the air. She looked at her brother. She knew he was as miserable as she was. "Wait here," he said. "I have an idea." In minutes he was back, carrying a pad of paper, a pen, an empty bottle and a shovel.

"What's all that for?" Hana asked.

"Maybe if we write down all the things that are bothering us," he said, "it'll help us feel better."

"That's stupid," Hana replied. "It won't bring back the park or the playground. It won't bring back Maria."

But George insisted. He was, after all, the big brother, and Hana didn't have a better idea. And so for the next several hours, the children poured their unhappiness onto paper, with George doing most of the writing and Hana doing much of the talking. They made lists of things they missed, lists of things they were angry about. Then they made lists of all the things they would do, all the things they would have, and all the places they would go when these dark times were over.

A young Hana and her father.

When they were done, George took the sheets of paper, rolled them into a tube, stuffed them into the bottle and popped in the cork. Then the two of them walked back toward the house, stopping at the double swing. There, Hana dug a big hole. This would be a hiding place for some of their sadness and frustration. George placed the bottle at the bottom of the hole and Hana filled the space back up with earth. And when it was all over the world seemed a little lighter and brighter, at least for the day.

It was hard to make sense of everything that was happening. Especially now that the family radio was gone. Father and Mother had depended on hearing the eight o'clock news every night from London, England to keep them informed of Hitler's latest evil act. But Jews had been ordered inside their houses by eight. Listening to the radio was absolutely forbidden and the penalty for breaking any law was very severe. Everyone was afraid of being arrested.

Father hatched a plan, an ingenious way to get around the Nazi rules. He asked his old friend, the keeper of the big church clock, to do him a favor. Would he mind, Father asked, turning the clock back fifteen minutes in the early evenings? That way Father could rush to the neighbor's house, hear the news, and be safely home when the bell rang at eight (which was actually eight-fifteen). The Nazi guard who patrolled the town square didn't have a clue. And Father was thrilled that his scheme had worked. Unfortunately, the news he was able to hear on the radio was bad. Very bad. The Nazis were winning every battle, advancing on every front.

Hana and George.

Tokyo, March 2000

THERESIENSTADT. Now Fumiko and the children knew that Hana had come to Auschwitz from Theresienstadt. Fumiko was excited. This was the first solid piece of information she had found about Hana. The first clue.

Theresienstadt was the name that the Nazis gave to the Czech town of Terezin. It was a pretty little town, with two imposing fortresses, first built in the 1800s to hold military and political prisoners. After the Nazis invaded Czechoslovakia, they turned Terezin into the Theresienstadt ghetto — a walled, guarded, overcrowded prison town to hold Jews who had been forced to leave their homes. Over the course of World War Two, more than 140,000 Jews were sent here — 15,000 of them were children.

Fumiko stayed up late at night, her office a glow of light in the darkened Center, reading everything she could find about Theresienstadt.

She learned that terrible things had happened in Theresienstadt, and that over the course of a few years almost everyone in the ghetto was deported again, put on trains and sent off to the more terrible concentration camps in the east which were known to be death camps.

But Fumiko also learned that brave and inspiring things happened in Theresienstadt. Among the adults were some very special people — great artists, famous musicians, historians, philosophers, fashion designers, social workers. They were all in Theresienstadt because they were Jews. An astonishing amount of talent, training and knowledge was crowded inside the walls of the ghetto. Under the noses of the Nazis and at great risk, the inmates secretly plotted and established an elaborate schedule of teaching, learning, producing and performing for both adults and children. They were determined to remind their students that — despite the war, despite the drab, cramped surroundings, despite everything — the world was a place of beauty and every individual person could add to it.

Fumiko also discovered that children in Theresienstadt were taught to paint and draw. And, miraculously, 4,500 drawings created by these children had survived the war. Fumiko's heart began to beat more quickly. Could it be that among those drawings there might be one or more by Hana Brady?

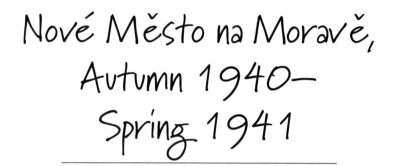

Nové Město na Moravě, Autumn 1940– Spring 1941

AUTUMN BROUGHT WITH IT A CHILL IN THE AIR, as well as more restrictions, and hardship.

Hana was about to begin grade three, when the Nazis announced that Jewish children would no longer be allowed to go to school. "Now, I will never see my friends!" Hana wailed, when her parents told her the bad news. "Now, I'll never become a teacher when I grow up!" She always dreamed of standing up at the front of the classroom and having everyone listen carefully to whatever she had to say.

Mother and Father were determined that both Hana and her brother would continue their education. Luckily, they had enough money to hire a young woman from the next village to be Hana's tutor, and an old refugee professor to teach George.

Mother tried to be cheerful. "Good morning, Hana," she would sing out when the sun rose. "It's time for breakfast. You don't want to be late for 'school.'" Every morning, Hana would meet her new tutor at the dining room table. She was a kind young woman and she did her best to encourage Hana with reading, writing and

Hana, her mother and George in happier times.

arithmetic. She brought a small blackboard that she leaned up against a chair. Once in a while, she allowed Hana to draw with the chalk and bang out chalk dust in the brushes. But at this school, there were no playmates, no practical jokes, no recess. Hana found it harder to pay attention or stay focused on her lessons. In the darkness of the winter, the world seemed to be closing in on the Brady family.

Indeed, when spring came, disaster struck. In March 1941, Mother was arrested by the Gestapo, Hitler's feared secret state police.

A letter came to the house ordering Mother to appear at nine o'clock in the morning at Gestapo headquarters in the nearby town of Iglau. In order to be there on time, she would have to leave in the middle of the night. She had one day to organize everything and say goodbye to her family.

She called Hana and George into the living room, sat on the couch, and pulled the children close to her. She told them that she would be going away for a while. Hana snuggled a little closer. "You must be good while I am gone," she said. "Listen carefully to Father and obey him. I will write," she promised. "Will you write back to me?"

George looked away. Hana trembled. The children were too shocked to reply. Their mother had never left them before.

When Mother tucked Hana into bed that night, she held her tightly. Mother ran her soothing fingers through Hana's hair, just the way she had when Hana was very little. She sang Hana's favorite lullaby, over and over again. Hana fell asleep with her arms around her mother's neck. In the morning when Hana woke up, Mother was gone.

Tokyo,
April 2000

FUMIKO COULD HARDLY BELIEVE IT when a flat package arrived at her office in Tokyo. Just a few weeks earlier, she had written to the Terezin Ghetto Museum in what is now called the Czech Republic. Fumiko had explained in her letter how anxious she and the children were to find anything that would connect them more closely to Hana. People there said they knew nothing about Hana's personal story. But they did know about the huge collection of children's drawings that had been hidden in the camp. Many of the drawings were now displayed at the Jewish Museum in Prague.

Fumiko opened the package. She was so excited that her hands were shaking. There were photographs of five drawings. One was a colored drawing of a garden and a park bench. Another showed people having a picnic beside a river. The rest were in pencil and charcoal, one of a tree, another of farmhands drying hay in a field, and another of stick people carrying suitcases, getting off a train. In the top right hand corner of each of the drawings was the name "Hana Brady."

One of Hana's drawings from Theresienstadt.

Nové Město na Moravě, Autumn 1941

SINCE SHE HAD MADE A PROMISE TO HER MOTHER, Hana did her best to behave well. She helped her father when she could and did her lessons. Boshka, their much-loved housekeeper, tried to cook Hana's favorite meals and give her extra helpings of dessert. But Hana missed her mother terribly, especially at night. No one else could smooth her hair with quite the same touch. No one else could sing her lullaby. And that big booming laugh of her mother's — everyone missed that.

The children learned that their mother was in a place called Ravensbruck, a women's concentration camp in Germany. "Is it far away?" Hana asked her father.

"When is she coming home?" George wanted to know. Father assured the children that he was doing everything he could to get her out.

One day Hana was reading in her room when she heard Boshka calling for her. She decided to ignore her. Hana didn't feel like doing any chores. And what else was there to look forward to? But Boshka kept calling. "Hana, Hana? Where are you? Come quickly! There is something very special waiting for you at the post office."

When she heard that, Hana dropped her book. Could it be what she hoped for most? She burst out of the house and ran down the street to the post office. Hana approached the wicket. "Do you have something for me?" she asked. The woman behind the counter slid a small brown package through the hole. Hana's heart leapt when she recognized her mother's writing. Her fingers trembled as she opened it. Inside was a little brown heart. It was made of bread and had the initials "HB" carved into it. Attached was a letter.

> *My dearest one, I wish you all the best on your birthday. I am sorry that I can't help you blow out the candles this year. But the heart is a charm I made for your bracelet. Are your clothes getting too small for you? Ask Daddy and Georgie to speak to your aunts about having some new ones made for my big girl. I think about you and your brother all the time. I am well. Are you being a good girl? Will you write me a letter? I hope you and George are keeping up your studies. I am well. I miss you so much, dearest Hanichka. I am kissing you now.*
> *Love, Mother. May 1941. Ravensbruck.*

Hana closed her eyes and clutched the little brown bread heart. She tried to imagine that her mother was standing beside her.

That fall brought another blow. One day Father arrived home carrying three squares of cloth. On each was a yellow star of David and in the middle of the star one word: *"Jude"* — Jew.

"Come children," said Father, as he took a pair of scissors from a kitchen drawer. "We need to cut out these stars and pin them on our coats. We must wear them whenever we leave the house."

"Why?" asked Hana. "People already know we are Jews."

"It's what we must do," replied Father. He looked so dejected, sad and tired that Hana and George didn't argue.

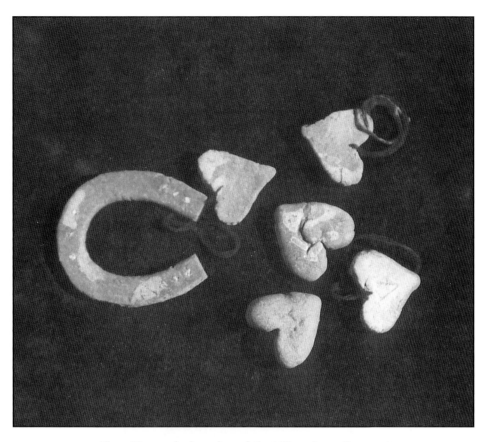

*The gifts made from bread that Hana's mother sent
to the family after she was taken away.*

From that day on, Hana went outside less often. She would do almost anything to avoid wearing the yellow badge in public. She hated the star. It was so humiliating. It was so embarrassing. Wasn't it enough, the children wondered, that they'd lost their park, their pond, their school and their friends? But now, when they left the house, the star was pinned to their clothing.

One Jewish man in town was not willing to obey. He'd had enough of all the rules and restrictions. So on a late September day in 1941, he left his house feeling a little brazen. He did not cut out the star and pinned the entire cloth to his coat. This tiny act of rebellion was immediately noticed by the Nazi officer in charge in Nové Město na Moravě. He was furious. He declared that Nové Město na Moravě must be made *judenfrei,* free of Jews, immediately.

The very next morning, a big black car driven by a Nazi officer drew up in front of the Bradys' house. Four frightened Jewish men were already huddled inside it. There was a knock on the door. Father opened it. Hana and George hung behind him. The Gestapo officer barked at Father to come out immediately. Hana and George couldn't believe their ears. They stood there, stunned, terrified and silent. Father hugged the children, implored them to be brave. And then he, too, was gone.

Jews were ordered to wear yellow cloth stars whenever they went out in public.

Tokyo, Spring 2000

FUMIKO WAS ENCHANTED BY HANA'S DRAWINGS. She knew they would help children better imagine what kind of person Hana had been. It would be easier for them to put themselves in her shoes. Fumiko was right.

More than ever, the children who volunteered at the Center focused their attention on Hana. Led by Maiko, some of them

Another of Hana's drawings from Theresienstadt.

formed a group with a mission to let other kids know about what they were learning. They called their club "Small Wings." Once a month, they met to plan their newsletter. Everyone had a role. The older kids wrote articles. The youngest were encouraged to draw pictures. Others wrote poems. With Fumiko's help, they sent their newsletter to schools far and wide, so others could find out about the history of the Holocaust and the search for Hana.

More than anything, they wanted to know what Hana looked like. They wanted to see the face of this little girl whose story they yearned to know. Fumiko realized that if she could find a photograph of Hana, she would be even more alive to the children as a real human being. Fumiko was determined that the search would continue.

Now that she had the drawings, a sock, the shoe, the sweater, and, of course, Hana's suitcase, Fumiko felt it was time to open the exhibit she had been working towards, "The Holocaust Seen Through Children's Eyes."

The Small Wings

Nové Město na Moravě, Winter 1941—1942

NOW THERE WERE ONLY TWO CHILDREN. No parents. George put an arm around his ten-year-old sister and promised to take care of her. Boshka, the housekeeper, tried to distract them with special treats and lighthearted talk. It didn't work. The children were sad and they were very scared.

Hours after their father's arrest there was another knock at the door. Hana's heart pounded. George swallowed hard. Who have they come for now? But when the children opened the door, they found Uncle Ludvik, their beloved Uncle Ludvik. "I've just heard the bad news," he said, hugging Hana with one arm, George with the other. "You are both coming with me. You belong with family, with people who love you."

Uncle Ludvik was a Christian who had married Father's sister. Because he wasn't Jewish, he was not an obvious target for the Nazis. But he was a brave man to take in George and Hana. The Gestapo had warned that terrible harm could come to anyone who helped the Jews.

Uncle Ludvik told the children to gather up their most treasured things. Hana took her life-sized doll named Nana whom she had had since she was five. George put together all the family photographs. Each of them filled a suitcase with clothes. Hana chose a

A younger Hana with George and her doll, Nana, that was almost as big as Hana herself.

large brown suitcase that she had taken before on family trips. She loved the polka-dot lining. When everything was packed, they turned out the light and closed the door behind them.

That night, her aunt and uncle tucked Hana into a big bed with a feather-filled comforter. "We will care for you until your parents come back, Hana," they promised. "And we'll be just down the hall, if you wake up in the night."

But long after lights out, Hana lay awake, blinking into the unfamiliar darkness. It was a strange bed. And the world — now full of danger — seemed to have turned upside down. What will come next? Hana wondered with fear. Finally, she closed her eyes and fell asleep.

Hana awoke the next morning to urgent barking outside her window. Her heart pounded. What could be wrong? Then she recognized the sounds. It was Sylva, their loyal wolfhound. She had found her way across town to be with Hana and George. At least some friends, Hana thought, stay true. It was a small comfort.

Aunt Hedda and Uncle Ludvik's house was small but comfortable, with a pretty little garden in the back. It was very close to the neighborhood school, and every day George and Hana watched the other children with their book bags, laughing, playing, on their way to their classes. "I want to go too!" Hana stamped her foot in hurt and frustration. But there was nothing anyone could do.

In the months that followed, Uncle Ludvik and Aunt Hedda did their best to keep the children busy. George chopped wood for hours on end. Hana read books and played games. She was well liked by her cousins Vera and Jiri. Sometimes she even went to church with them.

And every day at lunchtime, Hana and George went back to their old home to eat a familiar meal with their housekeeper, Boshka, who pampered them, hugged and kissed them, and reminded them that she had promised their parents that she would keep them healthy by feeding them well.

Every few weeks a letter would arrive from Father, who was imprisoned in the Iglau Gestapo prison. George would read only the cheerful part to his sister. George thought Hana was too young to know the whole truth about the harsh conditions in prison and how desperate Father was to be free. She was not too young, though, to be deported by the Nazis.

Hana, George and their wolfhound, Sylva.

Hana and her loving and brave Uncle Ludvik.

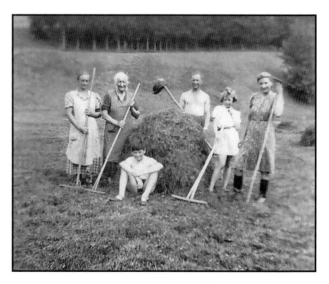

Hana and George helping out in the fields.

Nové Město na Moravě, May 1942

ONE DAY, A NOTICE WAS DELIVERED to Aunt Hedda and Uncle Ludvik's house. Hana and George Brady were ordered to report to a deportation center at Trebic, fifty kilometers away from Nové Město na Moravě, on May 14, 1942. This was what Uncle Ludvik had feared. He called Hana and George into his study and read them the letter. Then he tried to put the bad news in the best possible light. "You're going on a trip," he told them. "Together! You'll be going to a place where there are lots of other Jews, lots of other children to play with. Maybe there you won't have to wear the star!" George and Hana said very little. They were both unhappy about being uprooted again and leaving their aunt and uncle.

Hana was scared. When Boshka came to help them prepare for this strange trip, Hana peppered her with questions. "Where are our parents? When will we see them again? Where will we end up? What can we take with us?" Boshka didn't have any answers. The housekeeper told Hana that she, too, would be leaving Nové Město na Moravě to stay with a brother who lived on a farm.

Hana took out the large brown suitcase with the polka-dot paper lining from under her bed. She packed a sleeping bag that she hoped would give her the smell of home, no matter how far

JÜDISCHE KULTUSGEMEINDE IN PRAG
ŽIDOVSKÁ NÁBOŽENSKÁ OBEC V PRAZE

> Herrn, Frau, Fräulein
> Pan, paní, slečna
>
> *Brady Hanna*
>
> 100.436
>
> *Neustadtl Žďár*
>
> 13

Diese Vorladung ist mit Genehmigung der Zentralstelle für jüdische Auswanderung Prag (Dienststelle des Befehlshabers der Sicherheitspolizei beim Reichsprotektor in Böhmen und Mähren) als Reisegenehmigung anzusehen.	Tato obsílka platí za cestovní povolení na základě schválení Zentralstelle für jüdische Auswanderung Prag (Dienststelle des Befehlshabers der Sicherheitspolizei beim Reichsprotektor in Böhmen und Mähren).
Über Weisung der Zentralstelle für jüdische Auswanderung Prag haben Sie sich	Z nařízení Zentralstelle für jüdische Auswanderung Prag dostavíte se

am - dne **30. IV. 1942**

um - v **10** Uhr - hod.

in - do *Trebitsch*
einzufinden.

Jede vorgeladene Person hat mitzubringen	Každá předvolaná osoba přinese s sebou
1. Geburtschein,	1. rodný list,
2. Bürgerlegitimation (Kennkarte oder einen anderen Beleg über die Staatsbürgerschaft),	2. občanskou legitimaci (průkaz totožnosti nebo jiný úřední doklad o státní příslušnosti),
3. diese Vorladung.	3. toto předvolání.
Neben diesen Personaldokumente hat jede Person sämtliche Lebensmittelkarten mitzubringen.	Kromě těchto osobních dokladů, přinese každá osoba všechny potravinové lístky s sebou.

Um die vorgeschriebene Vorladungsstunde einhalten zu können, werden Sie den	Abyste dodržel(a) hodinu, na kterou jste byl(a) předvolán(a), použijete vlaku, který odjíždí

29.4.42 um - v **18.03** Uhr - hod.

von - z *Neustadtl über Saar*

abgehenden Zug benützen.

Zur Rückreise müssen Sie, den	K návratu musíte nastoupiti do vlaku, který opouští

um - v **16.38** Uhr - hod.

vom Vorladungsort abgehenden Zug benützen.   místo předvolání.

Kinder bis zu 4 Jahren müssen nicht persönlich erscheinen, doch müssen ihre Eltern oder verantwortl. Aufseher, sowohl die Personaldokumente, als auch diese Vorladung und die Lebensmittelkarte vorlegen. Kranke und alte Personen, die nicht persönlich erscheinen können, müssen neben allen Dokumenten ein amtsärztliches Zeugnis vorlegen lassen. Dieses Zeugnis muß eine genaue Diagnose der Krankheit enthalten.	Děti do 4 let se nemusí osobně dostaviti, avšak jejich rodiče nebo jejich zodpov. dozorce musí předložiti jak jejich osobní doklady, tak i toto předvolání a všechny potravinové lístky. Nemocné a staré osoby, které se nemohou osobně dostaviti, dají za sebe předložiti všechny doklady a mimo to vysvědčení úředního lékaře. Toto vysvědčení musí obsahovati přesnou diagnosu nemoci.

JÜDISCHE KULTUSGEMEINDE IN PRAG
ŽIDOVSKÁ NÁBOŽENSKÁ OBEC V PRAZE

This document orders Hana to be deported from her uncle's home on April 30, 1942. In fact, she was sent to Theresienstadt on May 14.

away they were sent. So did George. There was salami and sugar to tuck in amongst the clothes, as well as a few keepsakes.

Uncle Ludvik was heartbroken about sending his young niece and nephew away. He asked a driver to take them to the deportation center. Uncle Ludvik just couldn't face it himself. He and his wife did their best to hide their tears as they said goodbye to Hana and George. They promised to wait for their return to Nové Město na Moravě after the war was over. When the driver rang his bells, and the horses pulled away from the house, no one spoke a word.

A few hours later, the driver dropped Hana and George off in front of a huge warehouse. They joined the lineup near the entrance. When they reached the registration desk, they gave their names to a frowning soldier. He waved them into the dark, airless building.

The floor inside the building was covered with mats. Hana and George found two mats together in a corner and sat down. When they looked around, they realized there were hardly any other children. But there were hundreds of Jewish men and women, waiting to be sent to a place called Theresienstadt. They were all being deported.

For four days and four nights, Hana and George stayed in the warehouse, eating the food from their suitcases, sleeping on the mats. Though some of the adults tried to be kind to the children, Hana and George were not in a mood for company. They had each other and they passed the time reading, talking, napping and thinking of home. It was in this warehouse on May 16, 1942, with a few candies and a stub of a candle, that Hana Brady celebrated her eleventh birthday.

Tokyo, June 2000

THE EXHIBITION "THE HOLOCAUST SEEN THROUGH CHILDREN'S EYES" drew more visitors, adults and children alike, than Fumiko had dreamed possible. The story of the Holocaust was new to many of the people who came to the Museum. As Fumiko had hoped, its tragedy was made real for them by the objects she had gathered and the story they told.

Though they were interested in the shoe, the can of Zyklon B gas, and the little sweater, it was the suitcase that became a magnet. Children and their parents constantly gathered around it and examined the writing: Hana Brady, May 16, 1931, *Waisenkind* — orphan. They read the poems written by the members of Small Wings. And they admired the drawings Hana had made in Theresienstadt. "Do you know any more about her?" they asked. "What happened to her? What did she look like?" Fumiko decided to re-double her efforts to find a picture of Hana. Somewhere, someone had to be able to help them. Fumiko wrote back to the Terezin Ghetto Museum. No, came the answer. We already told you. We know nothing about a girl named Hana Brady.

Fumiko just couldn't accept this. She decided to go to Terezin herself.

Deportation Center, May 1942

ON THE MORNING OF THE FOURTH DAY, a loud whistle blew, and a Nazi soldier marched into the warehouse. Hana and George huddled in their corner as he barked out the orders.

"Everyone is to appear at the train tracks in one hour. Each person is allowed one suitcase. Twenty-five kilos. Not a gram more. Form straight lines. No talking. Do as you are told."

The voice was so harsh, so scary. Hana and George quickly got their things together. Adults tried to help them, making sure the children were ready. Poor little ones, they thought. Such a hard journey and alone, with no parents.

Under the threatening eyes of the soldiers, they all left the warehouse in single file and lined up at the tracks. From the brilliant sunlight of the morning, Hana and George stepped into the dark train, carrying their suitcases. More people piled in after them, until it was full. Then the doors slammed shut and the train began to move.

Terezin, July 2000

THERESIENSTADT. The name the Nazis gave the Czech town of Terezin. Fumiko knew that to solve the mystery of Hana's suitcase, she had to get there. But how? The Czech Republic was thousands of miles from Japan and a plane ticket would cost a lot of money that Fumiko didn't have.

But this time luck was on her side. Fumiko was invited to attend a conference on the Holocaust in England. From there, it would only be a short plane trip to Prague, capital of the Czech Republic. From Prague it was just a two-hour drive to Terezin. Fumiko couldn't wait to leave.

On the morning of July 11, 2000, Fumiko got off the bus in the main square of Terezin. At first glance, it looked like an ordinary pretty town. There were wide streets lined with trees and well-kept three-story houses with flowered window boxes. But Fumiko hardly noticed. She had exactly one day to accomplish her mission. That night she would have to go back to Prague. Her plane for Japan was leaving the next morning.

Fumiko hadn't phoned ahead. She had no appointment at the Museum. But directly across from the main square, she saw a long two-story pale yellow building. This was the Terezin Ghetto Museum.

Fumiko opened the heavy front door and entered the cool foyer. It was eerily quiet. Where was everybody? She poked her head into a few of the offices off the main entranceway. They were empty. There seemed to be no one in the building.

What has happened? Fumiko wondered. Could it be that everyone is out at lunch? No, it's only ten o'clock in the morning. Fumiko went back out into the square and tapped the shoulder of a friendly looking man on a park bench. "Can you help me?" she asked. "I'm looking for someone to help me in the Museum."

"Oh, you won't find anyone there today, young lady. It's a holiday and all the people who work there are away celebrating," the man replied. "I'm afraid you're out of luck."

Fumiko went to modern-day Terezin.

Theresienstadt, May 1942

THE TRAIN TRIP WAS QUIET, UNEVENTFUL. People seemed to keep to themselves, lost in their own thoughts and fears about the future. After a few hours, the train came to an abrupt halt. The doors were flung open and the frightened passengers standing nearest to the doors could see the sign reading "Bohusovic Station." Hana squinted in the sunlight as she and George lugged their suitcases off the train. There, at the station, they were instructed to walk the rest of the way to the Theresienstadt fortress.

It was only a few kilometers, but their suitcases were cumbersome and heavy. Should we leave some things here, Hana and George wondered, to lighten our load? No, everything in their suitcases was precious, the only reminders of the life they used to have. George carried one suitcase. The other one they put on a moving cart, pushed by prisoners.

Hana and George approached the entrance to the walled fortress and joined a lineup. Everyone was wearing a yellow star, just like them.

At the front of the line, a soldier asked people for their name, age and place of birth. Boys and men were being sent in one direction, girls and women in another. "Where are they going?" Hana asked George. More than anything else, she was afraid of being separated from her brother. "Can I stay with you?" she pleaded.

"Be quiet, Hana!" George told his sister. "Don't make a fuss."

When they reached the front of the line, the soldier stared at them. "Where are your parents?" he demanded.

"They are, uh, in another, uh, camp," George stammered. "We hope that here we might be reunited."

The soldier wasn't interested in conversation. He wrote down their names on index cards and searched their suitcases for money and jewellery. Then he slammed the bags shut. "To the left!" he ordered George. "To the right!" he ordered Hana.

"Please can I stay with my brother?" Hana asked.

"Move! Now!" the soldier ordered. What Hana feared most was about to happen. George gave her a quick hug. "Don't worry," he said. "I'll find you as soon as I can." Holding back tears, Hana picked up her suitcase and followed the other girls to *Kinderheim* (children's home) L410, a large barrack for girls that was to be Hana's home for the next two years.

Hana drew this picture of people getting off a train while she was at Theresienstadt.

Terezin, July 2000

FUMIKO COULDN'T BELIEVE IT. She was very upset — with herself and with her bad luck. I've come all this way and everyone who might be able to help me is on holiday. How did I manage to pick such a bad time to come to the Terezin Museum? How could I be so stupid? she thought. What do I do now?

As the hot sun beat down on her, a tear of frustration rolled down Fumiko's cheek. She decided to go back inside the Museum to try and collect her thoughts. Maybe she could come up with a different plan.

As she sat on a bench in the foyer, she heard a rustling sound. It appeared to be coming from one of the offices at the end of the hall. Fumiko tiptoed in the direction of the sound. There, in the last office on the right, she found a woman with glasses perched on the end of her nose, sorting through a huge stack of papers.

Startled, the woman almost jumped out of her chair when she saw Fumiko. "Who are you?" she asked. "What are you doing here? The Museum is closed."

"My name is Fumiko Ishioka," she replied. "I have come a long way from Japan to find out about a little girl who was here in Theresienstadt. We have her suitcase in our museum in Tokyo."

"Come back another day," the woman replied politely, "and someone will try and help you."

"But I don't have another day," exclaimed Fumiko. "My plane to Japan leaves tomorrow morning. Please," she pleaded. "Help me find Hana Brady."

The woman removed her glasses. She stared at the young Japanese woman and saw how anxious and determined she was. The Czech woman heaved a sigh. "All right," she said. "I can't promise anything. But I'll try and help you. My name is Ludmila."

Theresienstadt, 1942–43

KINDERHEIM L410 WAS A LARGE PLAIN BUILDING with about ten dormitory rooms. Twenty girls slept in each room, on burlap mattresses filled with straw in three-tiered bunk beds. Before the war, the town had been home to 5,000 people. The Nazis crammed ten times that number of prisoners into the same space.

There was never enough room, never enough food, never a chance for a private moment. There were too many people, too many bugs and rats, and too many Nazis who patrolled the camp with cruel discipline.

In the beginning, Hana, as a younger child, was not allowed to leave the building. That meant she couldn't see George. He lived in Kinderheim L417, which was just for boys, a few blocks away. Hana missed him terribly, and constantly asked the older girls, who were allowed outside, for news of him. They took Hana under their wing. They felt sorry for her, alone in the world, without her mother and father, away from her brother.

Hana made friends with an older girl in the next bunk. Ella was short, dark and very lively. She had a ready laugh and was happy to spend time with a younger girl who looked up to her and whom she could comfort in difficult times.

The man who gave out tickets for food took a liking to Hana and worried about her health. He knew that Hana was always hungry. He kindly offered to sneak her extra tickets, for another ladle of watery soup, another hunk of black bread. Hana's stomach growled and her mouth watered at the prospect of more food. But each time the offer was made, she politely said no. She'd been warned by Ella and the other older girls that she would be in big trouble with the guards if she was caught breaking a rule.

Torn from their families, crammed into small spaces, with barely enough to eat, the girls set about trying to make the best of a very bad situation. The ones over fifteen worked in the garden, where fruits, vegetables and flowers were grown for the Nazi soldiers. Once in a while, Mr. Schwartzbart, who ran the garden, allowed Hana to come out with the working group and enjoy the fresh air and sun. Hana loved the chance to work in the garden with the older girls. And there was an added bonus. A green bean here, and a strawberry there, always managed to find its way into a hungry girl's mouth.

But for the most part, Hana had to stay with girls her own age or younger, and obey the supervisor assigned to her room. Every day, they dusted, cleaned and swept under the bunks. Dishes, as well as faces, were washed under a pump. And every day there were secret classes held in the attic of Kinderheim L410.

In music classes, the girls learned new songs. They sang softly so they wouldn't be heard by the guards. At the end of each class, one child was chosen to sing a favorite song from home. When it was Hana's turn, she always sang a song called "Stonozka," the centipede song.

> *Her life is not a piece of cake.*
> *Imagine how she suffers when*
> *She walks until her tootsies ache.*

She's got good reason to complain.
So when I want to cry the blues
I just recall the centipede.
Consider walking in her shoes
And then my life seems sweet indeed.

There were sewing classes, too. Hana had never sewn a stitch in her life, and she had a hard time with the needle. The teacher often had to ask Hana to stop giggling when she made a silly mistake. Nonetheless she managed to finish a blue blouse of which she was very proud.

But Hana's favorite class was her art class. Painting and drawing supplies were hard to come by. Some people had smuggled them into the ghetto in suitcases. Paper had been stolen, sometimes at great risk, from the Nazi storerooms. Plain wrapping paper was used when nothing else could be found. One way or another, in the early days, there were always crayons and colored pencils.

The art teacher, Friedl Dicker-Brandeis, had been a famous painter and was now a fellow prisoner at Theresienstadt. Friedl taught her students about serious things like perspective and texture. And sometimes the girls drew pictures of serious subjects: the ghetto walls, people waiting in line for food, inmates being beaten by Nazi soldiers.

But, more than anything, Friedl wanted her classes to help the children forget their brutal surroundings, at least for a while. "Think of space," she told Hana and the others. "Think of freedom. Let your imagination run wild. Tell me what is in your hearts. Put it down on paper."

For a treat, she would take them to the roof of the building, so they could be closer to the sky. From there, they could look beyond the walls of the camp and see the surrounding moun-

Hana's drawing of people having a picnic under an umbrella, beside a river.

tains in the distance. The girls could dream of birds and butterflies, of ponds and swings. And, using their crayons and pencils, they could bring them to life.

When classes were over and all the chores were done, they played a board game called *Smelina*, which had been invented right there in the ghetto. It was based on Monopoly, created for the children by an engineer named Oswald Pock who had been deported to Terezin. The players would land on properties like *Entwesung*, the de-lousing station where clothes were disinfected, and the guards' barracks. Instead of building a hotel, players built a *kum-*

bal, an attic hideaway above the barracks. For money, players used the ghetto paper bills called ghetto *kronen.*

But no matter what the distractions, Hana always ended up feeling hungry and lonely. She missed George terribly. Then one day there was an announcement that the ghetto rules were changing. The girls were allowed to go out once a week for two hours.

Hana immediately raced across the square to the Boys' House. "George, George Brady!" she called. "Where is my brother? Have you seen my brother?" She ran from room to room, asking every boy she came across. So anxious was Hana to find her brother that she even opened the door to a bathroom. And there was George, working away at his new job as a plumber. What a joyous reunion it was! George threw down his tools and Hana rushed into his arms. They laughed. They cried. Questions tumbled from their mouths. "Are you well? Have you heard anything about Mother and Father? Are you getting enough to eat?" From then on, they took advantage of every opportunity to be together.

George took his responsibility as a big brother seriously. He felt it was his job to protect Hana and to make sure she didn't get into trouble. He wanted to keep her as happy and healthy as possible until they could be with their parents again.

And Hana was equally devoted to George. In Terezin, where there was never enough to eat, residents received a small *buchta,* a plain doughnut, once a week. Hana never ate hers. She brought it to George so he could be strong and stay sweet.

In Theresienstadt, it seemed to Hana that more people arrived every day. Men, women and children came from all over Czechoslovakia at first, and then from other European countries. Every time a new group of people got off the trains, Hana would look for familiar faces. And sometimes, when she was feeling strong, she would approach strangers and ask, "Do you know my mother and father? Have you been to a place called Ravensbruck? My mother is there! Do you have any news of Karel and Marketa Brady?" The answer was always the same, but delivered with kindness and a barely concealed pity. "No dear, we don't know your mother and father. But if we hear anything — anything at all — we will find you and tell you."

Then one day, a familiar face did appear — an old friend of her parents who had no children of her own. At first, Hana was thrilled to see her. Anything that reminded Hana of home, that brought her a tiny step closer to her mother and father, was a comfort. But suddenly it seemed that wherever Hana went, the woman was waiting for her. Every time Hana turned a corner, she was there. She pinched Hana's cheek, gave her kisses. And then one day, she went too far.

"Come here, little one," she said, holding her hand out. "Remember all our good times together. Don't be shy. Don't be lonely. You can come and see me every day. You can call me 'mother.' "

"I have a mother," Hana spat out. "Go away! Leave me alone." Hana refused to see the woman again. She missed her own mother. No one could take her place.

Terezin, July 2000

AT THE TEREZIN GHETTO MUSEUM, Ludmila sat down behind her desk and stared at the young Japanese woman perched on the edge of the seat across from her. Fumiko's strong determination was written all over her face. She liked Fumiko and wanted to help her find out more about this girl, this Hana Brady.

She pulled a big book off the shelves. Inside were the names of the almost 90,000 men, women and children who had been imprisoned at Theresienstadt and transported to the east. They turned to the B's: Brachova, Hermina. Brachova, Zusana. Brada, Tomas. Bradacova, Marta. Bradleova, Zdenka.

"Here she is," cried Ludmila. And there she was: Hana Brady, May 16, 1931. "How can I find out more about her?" Fumiko asked.

"I wish I knew," Ludmila replied.

"But look," said Fumiko, pointing to another line in the book. There was another Brady, listed right over Hana. "Could this be her family?" Fumiko wondered aloud. Ludmila looked at the birth dates. Three years apart. "Yes," she said, "chances are very good that this was a brother. The Nazis listed families together."

There was something else that Fumiko noticed. Beside Hana's name was a check mark. In fact, there was a check mark beside every name on the page — except one. Beside the other Brady, George Brady, there was nothing. What did this mean?

581	Wolfenstein Helone	Haushalt	15. 6. 1890	Gr. Meseritsch Oberstadt 350	100716
582	Wolfenstein Walter	Arbeiter	19.10. 1913	Gr. Meseritsch Oberstadt 350	100719
583	Wolfenstein Sidonie	Schneiderin	10. 4. 1911	Gr. Meseritsch Oberstadt 350	100718
584	Schück Ing. Friedrich	Masch.Ing.	23. 6. 1891	Unter Bobrau 81	100646
585	Drechsler Simon	Kaufmann	3. 8. 1833	Gr. Meseritsch Dalimilg.35	100483
586	Schnabel Rudolfine	Haushalt	20. 3. 1877	Unter Bobrau 81	100643
587	Schück MUDr. Ottokar	Arzt	4.11. 1894	Unter Bobrau 81	100649
588	Schück Edith	Haushalt	17. 6. 1907	Unter Bobrau 81	100647
589	Schück Ingmar	Schülerin	30. 3. 1930	Unter Bobrau 81	100645
590	Schück Zdenko	Schüler	31. 7. 1938	Unter Bobrau 81	100650
591	Fein Anna	Private	9. 6. 1890	Neustadtl 1.M.133	100491
592	Lauer Irma	Hausgehilfin	21. 8. 1933	Teltsch, Mladekgl81 dzt.Trebitsch Iglauer Vor 1	100117
593	Thierfeld Emma	Haushalt	13. 3. 1887	Stadt Saar 63	100636
594	Schwartz Irene H.	Fotografin	3.13. 1015	Stadt Saar 63	100634
595	Thierfeld Paul	Arbeiter	16. 3. 1936	Stadt Saar 63	100633
596	Brady Georg	Schüler	9. 2. 1928	Neustadtl 1.M.13	100435
597	Brady Hanna	Schülerin	16. 5. 1931	Neustadtl 1.M.13	100436
598	Jillisch Anna	Haushalt	27. 1. 1901	Dachesetz	100714
599	Blum Irene	Haushalt	25.10. 1891	Gr. Meseritsch Dalimilg.23	100433
600	Buchsbaum Elsa	Haushalt	13.13. 1892	Gr. Meseritsch Dalimilg.23	100448

From this list Fumiko learns that Hana had a brother.

Theresienstadt, 1943–44

As THE DAYS AND MONTHS PASSED, Theresienstadt became more crowded and cramped. New trainloads of people arrived all the time. This meant that there was less food for everyone and people became weak and sick. The oldest and youngest people were most at risk.

One day, after she had been in the ghetto for a year, Hana received an urgent message from her brother: Meet me at the Boys' House at six in the evening. I have a wonderful surprise for you.

George couldn't wait to share the good news. "Grandmother is here! She arrived last night!"

The children were overjoyed at the thought of seeing their grandmother. They were also worried. George and Hana's grandmother had been a refined woman who lived a cultured, comfortable life in the capital city of Prague. It was this generous grandmother who had given them their scooters. When they visited her in the big city, she always gave them bananas and oranges. But in recent years, she had been quite ill. How would she manage in this awful place? Not well, it turned out.

The children found her in an overcrowded attic, with only straw to sleep on, one of many old, sick people. It was the middle of July and the attic was boiling hot. They were horrified by what they saw. Their gentle, elegant grandmother looked terrible. Her

The now-renovated girls' barracks in Theresienstadt, where Hana lived.

beautiful white hair, always so perfectly combed in the past, was a mess. Her clothes were torn and soiled. "I've brought you one of my paintings," Hana exclaimed, thinking it might put a smile on the old woman's face. But her grandmother could barely turn her head. Instead Hana folded the coarse paper and made her painting into a fan. "Rest," she told her grandmother as she tried to create a cooling breeze. Hana felt proud to be in charge of trying to help her grandmother feel better.

Hana soon learned that old people in Theresienstadt were given the smallest and worst rations. The food her grandmother got just wasn't enough and was often crawling with bugs. And there was no medicine. The children visited as often as they could and tried to cheer her up, bringing crafts they'd made and singing songs they'd learned. "This bad time will all be over soon," George told her. "Mother and Father are counting on us all to stay strong," Hana said.

But in three months time, their grandmother was dead. Beyond Hana and George, few people took much notice. Death was all around them. In fact, so many people were dying so fast, the cemetery was full. Clinging to each other, Hana and George tried to remember the happy times with their grandmother, and cried together.

As more people poured into Terezin, thousands more poured out. They were crammed into boxcars and sent eastward to an unknown fate. Rumors about the transports spread inside the walls of Theresienstadt. Some tried to convince themselves and others that a better life awaited the people who were sent away on the trains. But as time went on, stories of death camps, brutality and mass murder circulated widely. When people spoke of these things, Hana covered her ears.

Every few weeks, the dreaded lists would be posted in each building. People whose names were on them had to report to an assembly hall close to the railway station within two days.

Lists. Everywhere there were lists. The Nazis were systematic record keepers and they wanted all their prisoners to know it. Through the constant counting and listing of people, the Nazis reminded the inmates who was in charge. Everyone knew that being counted, being noticed, could mean a transport and another separation from family and friends.

One morning, as Hana was doing her chores, everyone in the camp was ordered to stop what they were doing and assemble on a huge field outside the town. Everyone — old and young. They were marched out by Nazi guards carrying machine guns, and ordered to stand there with no food, no water, and a sense that something terrible was about to happen. Hana and the other girls didn't even dare to whisper among themselves.

Hana couldn't bear the thought that she might be separated from George. Or from the girls in Kinderheim L410, who had become almost like sisters. Wasn't it enough that her parents had been taken away from her? Ella stood beside her and tried to cheer her up with smiles and winks. But after four hours of standing, Hana could no longer contain her despair. She began to cry.

Ella slipped her a tiny piece of bread she had hidden in her coat. "Eat this, Hana," she quietly implored. "You will feel better." But Hana's tears kept coming. The big girl then turned to her. "Listen carefully to me," she whispered. "You are unhappy and scared. That's just how the Nazis want to see us, all of us. You can't give them the satisfaction, Hana. You can't give them what they want. We are stronger and better than that. You must dry up those tears, Hana, and put on a brave face." Miraculously, Hana did.

The Nazi commander began shouting out names. Everyone had to be accounted for. Finally, after eight hours of standing in a bitter wind, everyone was ordered to march back to the barracks.

It was September, 1944. When the Nazis began to realize that they were losing the war they announced that more people would be leaving Theresienstadt. The transports were sped up. Now a new list of names went up every day.

Each morning, her heart pounding, Hana ran down to the main entrance of the building where the list was posted. And one day there it was — the name she dreaded finding — George Brady. Hana's knees buckled. She sat down on the ground and cried. George, her beloved brother, her protector, was being sent away to the east. That wiry boy, now a young man, was told to report to the trains along with 2,000 other able-bodied men.

At their last meeting, on the dirt path between the Boys' House and Kinderheim L410, George asked Hana to listen carefully. "I leave tomorrow," he said. "Now, more than ever, you must eat as much as you can. You must breathe fresh air at every opportunity. You must take care of your health. Be strong. Here is my last ration. Eat every last crumb."

George gave Hana a huge bear hug and gently pushed the hair out of her eyes. "I promised Mother and Father that I would take care of you and bring you home safely so that we can all be together as a family again. I don't want to break that promise." Then the curfew whistle screamed and George was gone.

Hana became despondent. She couldn't bear the separation from her brother. First her parents, and now George. She felt so terribly alone in the world. Sometimes, when the other girls tried to cheer her up, Hana turned her face away or even snapped at them, "Can't you just leave me alone?"

Only gentle Ella could convince her to eat her meager rations. "Remember what your brother told you. You need to take care of yourself and stay strong — for him."

Four weeks later, Hana learned that she, too, was going east. A reunion! "I'll see George again," she told everyone. "He's waiting for me."

She sought out Ella. "Can you help me?" she asked. "I want to look nice when I see my brother. I want to show him how well I've taken care of myself." Despite her own fears, Ella wanted to nourish the hopes of her young friend. She smiled at Hana and set to work. She got water at the pump and used her last little square of soap to wash Hana's face and to clean her knotted, dirty hair. With a piece of rag she tied Hana's hair into a ponytail. She pinched Hana's cheeks to bring up a little red. Ella stood back and looked at the results of her efforts. Hana's face shone with hope. "Thank you Ella," Hana said, hugging the bigger girl. "I don't know what I would do without you." For the first time since George had been sent away, she looked happy.

That night, Hana packed her suitcase. There wasn't much to put into it: a few pieces of pretty worn out clothing, one of her favorite drawings from Friedl's art class, a book of stories that Ella had given her. When she was done, Hana got into her bunk and slept her last night in Theresienstadt.

The next morning, she and many of the other girls from Kinderheim L410 were marched out to the railroad track. Nazi guards barked orders and their dogs bared their teeth and growled. No one stepped out of line.

"Where do you think we are going?" Hana whispered to Ella. No one really knew. The girls boarded the darkened rail car one by one, until there was not an inch of room left in the train. The air turned sour. And the wheels began to turn.

The train chugged on for a day and a night. There was no food. There was no water. There was no toilet. The girls had no idea how long the journey would be. Their throats were parched, their bones ached, their stomachs twitched with hunger.

They tried to comfort each other, singing songs of home. "Lean on me," Ella said softly, "and listen, Hana."

> *So when I want to cry the blues*
> *I just recall the centipede.*
> *Consider walking in her shoes*
> *And then my life seems sweet indeed.*

The girls held hands. They closed their eyes and tried to imagine being somewhere else. Each girl imagined something different. When Hana closed her eyes, she saw the strong, smiling face of her brother.

And then suddenly, in the middle of the night on October 23, 1944, the wheels of the train ground to a screeching halt. The doors were opened. The girls were ordered out of the boxcar. This was Auschwitz.

An angry guard ordered them to stand straight and silent on the platform. He held tight the leash of a large dog straining to pounce. The guard looked the group up and down quickly. He cracked his whip in the direction of one girl who had always been embarrassed by how tall she was. "You," he said, "over there, to the right!" He cracked his whip one more time at another of the older girls. "You, there too." Then he called over to a group of young soldiers who stood at the edge of the platform. "Take them, now!" he ordered, pointing to Hana and the rest of her group. Huge searchlights almost blinded the girls. "Leave your suitcases on the platform," the soldiers commanded.

Through a wrought iron gate and under the watchful eyes of the surly dogs and uniformed men, Hana and her old roommates were marched off. Hana held on tight to Ella's hand. They passed huge barracks, saw the skeleton-like faces of prisoners in their striped uniforms peeking out the doors. They were ordered to enter a large building. The door closed behind them with a frightening bang.

Terezin, July 2000

"WHAT DOES THE CHECK MARK MEAN?" asked Fumiko, as she looked at the page listing Hana Brady and George Brady.

Ludmila hesitated and then spoke carefully. "The check mark means that the person didn't survive."

Fumiko lowered her eyes to the paper again. Hana's name had a check mark beside it. Like almost all the 15,000 children who passed through Theresienstadt, Hana had died at Auschwitz.

Fumiko bowed her head and closed her eyes. She had already guessed the awful truth. But hearing it spoken, seeing it on paper was still a blow. Fumiko sat silently for a few minutes, trying to take it all in.

And then she gathered herself together and looked up. Hana's story was not over. Now, more than ever, Fumiko wanted to know everything about her — for herself, for the children waiting for her back in Japan, and for Hana's memory. She was absolutely determined that this life, ended so unjustly, at such a young age, would not be forgotten. It had become her mission to make sure of this. The quest was not over.

"There is no check mark beside George's name," Fumiko said. "Is there any way," she stammered, "that we can find out about him? What happened to him? Where did he go? Is he still alive?"

If she could only find him, he might help her discover more about Hana. Fumiko began to tremble with excitement.

Ludmila looked sadly across the desk at Fumiko. She could see how badly Fumiko wanted to know. "I have no idea what happened to him," she said softly. "The war was such a long time ago, you know. He could have gone anywhere in the world. He could even have changed his name. Or he could have died, long after the war."

"Please," Fumiko pleaded, "you have to help me find him."

The woman sighed and turned back to the bookshelves crammed with bound volumes of names on lists. "We can keep looking for clues in here," she said. For an hour, Fumiko and Ludmila sorted through books filled with names, looking for another mention of George Brady. And finally, they found one.

He was on the list of inmates of Kinderheim L417, the Boys' House at Theresienstadt. The names were clumped in groups of six, since two boys shared each mattress in the three-tiered bunks. When Ludmila checked the names listed with George Brady, she looked up at Fumiko with a start.

"Kurt Kotouc," she said. "Kurt Kotouc," she repeated. "I know that name. He's alive. I think George Brady's bunkmate used to live in Prague, but I have no idea where. If we can locate him, maybe he can tell you what happened to Hana's brother. Unfortunately, there's nothing more I can do for you here. Try the Jewish Museum in Prague. Maybe someone there can help."

Fumiko thanked Ludmila over and over again for all she had done. She hugged her and promised to let her know about the results of her sleuthing. Ludmila wished Fumiko luck. Then Fumiko picked up her briefcase and ran out of the office into the town square. The bus for Prague was due at any moment.

Prague, July 2000

FUMIKO HAD ONLY A FEW HOURS OF DAYTIME remaining before her plane left for Japan early the next morning. As soon as she got off the bus in Prague, she hailed a taxi. "The Jewish Museum, please," she said, trying to catch her breath.

She arrived at the Prague Jewish Museum just before closing time. The guard told her to come back the next day. "But I can't," pleaded Fumiko. "I have to go back to Japan tomorrow morning. I'm here to see Michaela Hajek. She helped me find some very important drawings." When nothing else seemed to convince the guard, Fumiko bent the truth a little. "She's expecting me," Fumiko told the man confidently. And he let her in.

This time, luck was on Fumiko's side. The woman was in her office and remembered the story of Hana. She listened carefully as Fumiko explained what she had found out.

"I have heard of Kurt Kotouc," Michaela said quietly. Fumiko could barely believe it. "I will try and help you find him," Michaela promised. She understood that Fumiko had no time to lose.

Fumiko sat quietly as Michaela made phone call after phone call. Each person Michaela spoke to gave her another number to try and wished her well in the search. Finally she reached an office where Mr. Kotouc worked as an art historian. She handed the phone to Fumiko who tried to explain what she was looking for. The secretary wanted to help, but told her Mr. Kotouc was leaving on an overseas trip that evening. "I'm sorry," she said to Fumiko, "a meeting will be impossible." No, he didn't even have time for a phone call.

Michaela watched as Fumiko's face fell. She got back on the phone herself and pleaded with the secretary. "You have no idea how desperate this young woman is. She has to go back to Japan in the morning. This is her only chance." The secretary finally relented.

Two hours later, the sky was dark and the Museum was officially closed. All the staff had gone home. But one office was still brightly lit. There, Fumiko and Michaela awaited the arrival of Mr. Kotouc.

Finally he came. The heavyset man with bright eyes had much to tell. "I only have half an hour," he said, "before I leave for the airport. Of course, I remember George Brady. We shared a bunk in Theresienstadt and much more. You never forget the connections you make with people in a place like Theresienstadt. Not only that," he said, "we are still friends. He lives in Toronto, Canada."

Mr. Kotouc pulled out a small leather book. "Here's what you're looking for," he said with a smile.

He wrote down George Brady's address and gave it to Fumiko. "Oh, Mr. Kotouc, I can't thank you enough," Fumiko said.

"Good luck," he told Fumiko. "I'm so happy that children in Japan want to understand the lessons of the Holocaust." And then Mr. Kotouc practically flew out of the office, baggage in hand.

Fumiko beamed from ear to ear. All her persistence had paid off. She told Michaela how grateful she was for her help.

The next morning Fumiko settled in her seat for the long flight to Japan. She was still tingling with excitement. She tried to recall

all the news she had for the children at the Center. When she thought about Hana having a big brother, Fumiko couldn't help picturing her own little sister, three years younger. Fumiko had always been her protector and she tried to imagine what she would do if her little sister were in danger. The very thought made her shudder. She looked out the window as the story repeated itself over and over in her mind. After an hour, she fell into a deep sleep, the first one she'd had in a long time.

Tokyo, August 2000

BACK IN TOKYO, Fumiko called a special meeting of Small Wings. She shared every detail of her adventure with the members. The sad news came first. With the children around her in a circle, Fumiko told them, in a quiet voice, what they had already imagined. Hana had died at Auschwitz.

"But I have a wonderful surprise," Fumiko said. The faces of the children brightened. "Hana had a brother named George — and he survived!"

The questions started flying at once. "Where is he?" asked Maiko. "How old is he?" one boy wanted to know. "Does he know that we have Hana's suitcase?" asked Akira. Fumiko told them everything she knew. And she said she would work late that very night so that she could write George a letter.

"Can we send something with it?" asked Maiko. The older kids scattered to quiet spots around the Center to compose poems. "What can I do?" Akira asked Maiko.

"Draw a picture of Hana," she replied.

"But I don't know what she looks like," he said.

"Just draw her as you imagine her," Maiko said. And Akira did.

Fumiko wrote her own letter very carefully. She knew that receiving it would come as a shock to George. She knew that some

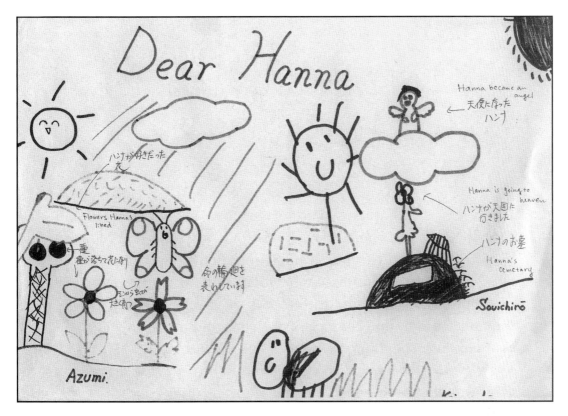

A tribute to Hana by children at the Holocaust Center. They used the German spelling of Hana's name because it was spelled that way on the suitcase.

Holocaust survivors refused to ever speak about their experiences. She worried that his memories might be so bitter and painful that he wouldn't want to hear anything about Hana's suitcase and the Holocaust Center in Japan.

Fumiko had copies made of Hana's drawings and packaged them carefully, along with the children's writings and artwork. Then she took the parcel down to the post office, crossed her fingers, and sent it off to Canada.

Toronto, Canada
August 2000

IT WAS A WARM AND SUNNY AUGUST AFTERNOON. Seventy-two-year-old George Brady had come home from work early and had planned to spend a quiet afternoon in the empty house, clearing up some bills. He was sitting at his dining room table when he heard the footsteps of the mailman, the whoosh of envelopes being shoved through the slot, and the thunk of them landing on the floor. I'll get them later, he thought. Then the doorbell rang.

When he opened the door, the mailman was standing there. "This wouldn't fit through," he said, handing a package to George. The package was postmarked Japan. What could this be? George wondered. He didn't know anyone in Japan.

When he opened the package and began to read the letter, George's heart began to pound. He closed his eyes. He opened them, blinking hard, making sure that what he was reading was real. Was this a daytime dream he was having?

The loss of his sister Hana was George's most private and deepest sorrow. He had lived with it for over half a century and had never been able to get over the feeling that he should have been able to protect his little sister.

Now, somehow, halfway around the world, her story was being told and her life was being honored. George was stunned. He sat down and let his mind wander back fifty-five years.

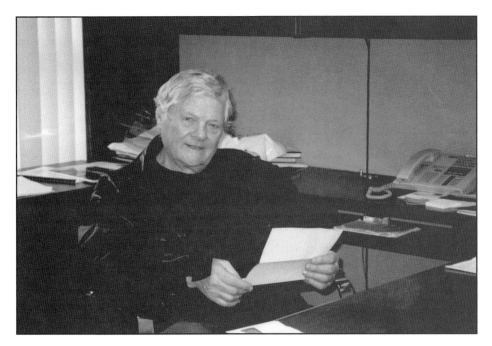

George Brady today.

When Auschwitz was liberated in January 1945, George Brady was seventeen years old. He had survived the horrors of the camp by starting out young and strong, by good luck, and by using the trade he had learned at Theresienstadt — plumbing. When he was freed, he was very weak and painfully thin. But George was determined to make his way back to Nové Město na Moravě — to his parents and his little sister Hana. He desperately wanted his family to be together again.

By foot, by train and by hitchhiking, George made it back to the home he loved in May 1945. He went straight for Uncle Ludvik and Aunt Hedda's house. It was the last place where he had known family, love and safety. When they opened the door and found their nephew standing there, aunt and uncle fell on him — hugging, kissing, touching, crying — barely able to believe that George was alive.

But the unbridled happiness of the reunion was short-lived. "Where are Mother and Father?" George asked. Ludvik and Hedda were forced to tell him the terrible truth. Marketa had been sent from Ravensbruck to Auschwitz and murdered there in 1942. Karel was killed there the same year. "And Hana?" George whispered. All his aunt and uncle knew was that she had been sent to Auschwitz.

For months, George nursed the faint hope that somehow, somewhere, Hana would appear. He searched for her in every young girl's face he saw, in every ponytail that swished by, in every jaunty step of a healthy child on the street. One day, George encountered a teenaged girl on the main street in Prague. She stopped in front of him.

"George?" she asked. "Are you not George Brady, Hana's brother? My name is Marta. I knew Hana. All of us older girls at Theresienstadt loved her." George searched Marta's eyes for information, for hope. She realized that George didn't yet know the final truth about his sister. "George," she told him quietly, plainly, taking hold of his hands. "Hana was sent to be killed in the gas chamber at Auschwitz, the same day she arrived there. I'm sorry, George. Hana is dead." George's knees turned to jelly and the world went black.

Toronto, August 2000

IN THE MORE THAN HALF A CENTURY since George learned the terrible fates of his parents and sister, much had happened. At seventeen, George had left Nové Město na Moravě. He moved from city to city in Europe, carrying his only treasured possession — the box of family photographs that Uncle Ludvik and Aunt Hedda had hidden for him. Then, in early 1951, he moved to Toronto and set up a plumbing business with another Holocaust survivor. It was very successful. George married, became the father of three sons and, much later, of a daughter.

George was proud that — despite his suffering during the Holocaust and the fact that his mother, father and sister had been murdered by the Nazis — he had moved on with his life. He was a successful businessman, a proud father. He thought of himself as a healthy person who, for the most part, put his wartime experiences behind him. But whatever he accomplished, whatever joy he felt, it was always tinged with the memory of his beautiful little sister and the horror of her fate.

And now, here he was, with a letter from halfway around the world, telling him how his sister's suitcase was helping a new generation of Japanese children learn about the Holocaust. The letter from Fumiko also asked, very gently, for his help.

〒160-0015 東京都新宿区大京町28-105
TEL:03-5363-4808 FAX:03-5363-4809

28-105 Daikyo-cho,Shinjuku-ku Tokyo,160-0015 JAPAN
TEL:+81-3-5363-4808 FAX:+81-3-5363-4809
E-mail:Holocaust@Tokyo.email.ne.jp
Homepage:http://www.ne.jp/asahi/holocaust/tokyo

ホロコースト教育資料センター
Tokyo Holocaust Education Resource Center

~For Children, Builders of Peace

Mr. George Brady
23 Blyth Hill Road
Toronto 12, M4N 3L5
CANADA

August 22, 2000

Dear Mr. Brady,

We take a liberty of addressing and telling you about our activities in Japan. My name is Fumiko Ishioka and I am Director of Tokyo Holocaust Education Resource Center. In July this year I met with Mr. Kurt Jiri Kotouc in Prague and I got your address from him. The reason why I am writing to you is because we are now exhibiting your sister, Hanna Brady's suitcase at our Center. Please forgive me if my letter hurts you reminding you of your past difficult experiences. But I would very much appreciate it if you could kindly spare some time to read this letter.

Please let me start with a little explanation on what we do in Japan. Tokyo Holocaust Education Resource Center, established in October 1998, is a non-profit, educational organization that aims at further promoting understanding of the history of the Holocaust especially among young children in this country. Children here do not have a chance to learn about the Holocaust, but we believe it is our responsibility too to let our next generation learn the lessons of the Holocaust so that such a tragedy would never be repeated again anywhere in the world. As well as learning the truth of the Holocaust, it is also very important for children, we believe, to think about what they can do to fight against racism and intolerance and to create peace by their own hands.

Besides welcoming children at our Center for exhibition and study programs, this year we organized a pair of traveling exhibition, "The Holocaust Seen Through Children's Eyes" in order to reach more children living far from our Center. For this project, we borrowed some children's memorial items from individuals and museums in Europe, one of which is Hanna Brady's suitcase from the museum of Auschwitz. Many children are now visiting our Center to see this suitcase to learn about the Holocaust. In June, furthermore, we held the Children's Forum on the Holocaust 2000, where our Center's children's group "Small Wings" did a little opening performance on Hanna's suitcase. "Small Wings" is a group of children, aged from 8 to 18, who write newsletters and make videos to let their friends know about the Holocaust and share what they learn from it. At the Forum they decided to use Hanna's suitcase to do an introduction for their friends who have never heard of the Holocaust. It successfully helped participants of the Forum focus on one little life, among one and a half million, lost during the Holocaust, and think about importance of remembering this history.

When I received the suitcase from the museum of Auschwitz, all the information I had were things written on the suitcase, her name and her birthday, and from the Terezin memorial book I got the date when she was deported to Auschwitz. I could also find 4 of her drawings from Terezin. But that was all. Hoping to get more information on Hanna, I went to Terezin in July, when I found your name on the list I got from the ghetto museum and heard that you survived. I was then so lucky to find Mr. Kotouc in Prague and met with him, from whom I heard you now live in Toronto. Those children of "Small Wings" were all so excited to know Hanna had a brother and he survived.

I was wondering if you would kindly be able to tell us about you and Hanna's story, the time you spent with Hanna before sent to the camp, things that you talked with her, you and her dreams, and anything that would help children here feel close to you and Hanna to understand what prejudice, intolerance and hatred did to young Jewish children. If possible, I would be grateful if you could lent us any kind of memorial items such as your family's photo, and so on. It will greatly help us further promote our goal to give every child in Japan a chance to learn about the Holocaust.

Thank you very much for your time. I would very much appreciate your kind understanding for our activities.

I look forward to hearing from you.

With kindest regards,

Fumiko Ishioka
Director
Tokyo Holocaust Education Resource Center

Fumiko's letter to George.

Please forgive me, if my letter hurts you by reminding you of your difficult experiences. But I would very much appreciate if you would kindly be able to tell us about your and Hana's story. We would like to know about the time you spent with Hana before you were sent to the camp, the things that you talked with her about, your and her dreams. We are interested in anything that would help children here in Japan feel close to you and Hana. We want to understand what prejudice, intolerance, and hatred did to young Jewish children.

If possible, I would also be grateful if you could lend us any family photos. I know that most Holocaust survivors lost their family photographs, along with their families. But if you do have any pictures, it would greatly help us with our goal to give every child in Japan a chance to learn about the Holocaust. We at the Tokyo Holocaust Center and the children of Small Wings are all so excited to know that Hana had a brother and that he survived.

It was signed "Fumiko Ishioka."

George could hardly believe it. Such amazing connections and strange coincidences had brought three worlds together: the world of children in Japan, George in Canada, and the lost world of a Jewish girl from Czechoslovakia who died so long ago. George wiped the tears from his cheek and then smiled to himself. Hana's young face was so clear to him. He could almost hear her laugh, and feel her soft hand in his. George went to the large wooden dresser and pulled out a photograph album. He wanted to get in touch with Fumiko Ishioka as soon as possible.

Tokyo, September 2000

EVER SINCE SHE HAD SENT THE LETTER TO TORONTO, Fumiko had been a bundle of nerves. Would George Brady write back? Will he help us to know Hana? Even the letter carrier who delivered the mail to the Center knew how anxious Fumiko was. "Anything from Canada today?" she would ask the minute she saw him walking up the path to the front door. He hated to see her disappointment when, day after day, the answer was no.

Then on the last day of the month, Fumiko was in the middle of welcoming forty guests at the Center. They were teachers and students who had come to learn about the Holocaust and to see the suitcase. Out of the corner of her eye, through a window, she saw the letter carrier walking very quickly toward the building with a huge smile on his face. Fumiko excused herself and ran to meet him. "Here it is," he said, beaming. And he handed her a thick envelope from Toronto.

"Oh thank you," Fumiko cried. "Thank you for making my day!"

She took the letter to her office and opened it. As she unfolded the pages, photos spilled out. Four photographs of Hana, her blonde hair shining around her smiling face.

Fumiko screamed. She couldn't help it. Some of the visiting teachers and students rushed to her office door. "What's wrong?

What's the matter?" they asked.

"Nothing is wrong," she told them, stumbling over her words. "I'm just so happy, so excited. Here, look, this is a picture of Hana. This is the beautiful little girl whose story we have worked so hard to find."

Along with the photographs, there was a long letter from George. In it, Fumiko learned about Hana's happy early days in Nové Město na Moravě, about her family, and how she loved to ski and skate. It was comforting to know that Hana had had a good life before the war ruined everything.

Hana

And Fumiko learned about George, too. As she read about his life in Canada, his children and his grandchildren, Fumiko was bursting with happiness. She began to cry. He survived, she repeated over and over to herself. He survived. More than that, he has a beautiful family. She couldn't wait to tell the children of Small Wings.

Tokyo, March 2001

"CALM DOWN," FUMIKO SAID WITH A SMILE. "They'll be here soon, I promise."

But nothing she said could tame the excitement of the children that morning. They buzzed around the Center, checked their poems, straightened their clothes for the umpteenth time, told silly jokes just to make the time move faster. Even Maiko, whose job it was to calm everyone else down, was jumpy.

Then, finally, the waiting was over. George Brady had arrived. And he had brought with him his seventeen-year-old daughter, Lara Hana.

Now the children became very quiet. At the Center's front entrance, they crowded around George. They bowed to him, as is the custom in Japan. George bowed back. Akira presented George with a beautiful multi-colored origami garland. All the children jostled gently for the chance to be nearest to him. After so many months of hearing about George from Fumiko, they were thrilled to finally meet him in person.

Fumiko took George's arm. "Come with us, now, and see your sister's suitcase." They walked to the display area.

And there, surrounded by the children, with Fumiko holding one of his hands and his daughter, Lara, holding the other, George saw the suitcase.

Photo: The Chugoku Newspaper

Fumiko holds a picture of the suitcase as George Brady talks to children during his trip to Japan and the Holocaust Center.

Suddenly, an almost unbearable sadness came over him. Here was the suitcase. There was her name written right on it. Hana Brady. His beautiful, strong, mischievous, generous, fun-loving sister. She had died so young and in such a terrible way. George lowered his head and let the tears flow freely.

But, a few minutes later, when he looked up, he saw his daughter. He saw Fumiko, who had worked so hard to find him and the story of Hana. And he saw the expectant faces of all those Japanese children for whom Hana had become so important, so alive.

George realized that, in the end, one of Hana's wishes *had* come true. Hana had become a teacher. Because of her — her suitcase and her story — thousands of Japanese children were learning about what George believed to be the most important values in the world: tolerance, respect, and compassion. What a gift Fumiko and the children have given me, he thought. And what honor they have given Hana.

Fumiko asked the children to sit in a circle. She beamed with pride as, one by one, they presented George with their drawings and poems about Hana. When they had finished, Maiko stood up, took a deep breath, and read a poem aloud.

> *Hana Brady, thirteen years old, was the owner of this*
> *suitcase.*
> *Fifty-five years ago, May 18, 1942 — two days after Hana's*
> *eleventh birthday — she was taken to Terezin*
> *in Czechoslovakia.*
> *October 23, 1944, crowded into the freight train, she*
> *was sent to Auschwitz.*
> *She was taken to the gas chamber right after.*
> *People were allowed to take only one suitcase with them.*
> *I wonder what Hana put in her suitcase.*
> *Hana would have been sixty-nine years old today, but*
> *her life stopped when she was thirteen.*
> *I wonder what kind of girl she was.*
> *A few drawings she made at Terezin — these are the*
> *only things she left for us.*
> *What do these drawings tell us?*
> *Happy memories of her family?*
> *Dreams and hopes for the future?*
> *Why was she killed?*
> *There was one reason.*

While Maiko reads on the left, members of the Small Wings hold up signs saying "Let's Learn, Think and Act [to create peace] for the 21st century."

She was born Jewish.
Name: Hana Brady. Date of Birth: May 16, 1931. Orphan.
We, Small Wings, will tell every child in Japan what happened to Hana.
We, Small Wings, will never forget what happened to one-and-a-half-million Jewish children.
We children can make a difference in building peace in the world — so that the Holocaust will never happen again.

By Small Wings, December 2000, Tokyo, Japan.
Translated from Japanese by Fumiko Ishioka.

Afterword

The story of *Hana's Suitcase* continues to hold surprises for us. On a trip to Poland in March 2004, George and Fumiko learned that Hana's original suitcase was destroyed, along with many other objects from the Holocaust, in a suspicious fire in Birmingham, England in 1984.

The museum at Auschwitz created a replica — or copy — of the suitcase from a photograph. It was that replica which Fumiko and the Small Wings received in Tokyo. As a matter of policy Auschwitz tells borrowers when an object on loan is not the original. This time a mistake was made. George and Fumiko did not know that the suitcase was a reproduction until the trip to Poland.

On reflection, everyone involved is grateful that the curators at Auschwitz went to the trouble of creating a faithful replica of the suitcase. Without it, Fumiko would never have searched for Hana. She would never have found George. And we would never have the story of *Hana's Suitcase*.

Hana's Suitcase is now being read around the world by hundreds of thousands of children, in more than twenty languages. Fumiko, George and the suitcase continue to travel, sharing Hana's story, the lessons of history and a message of tolerance.

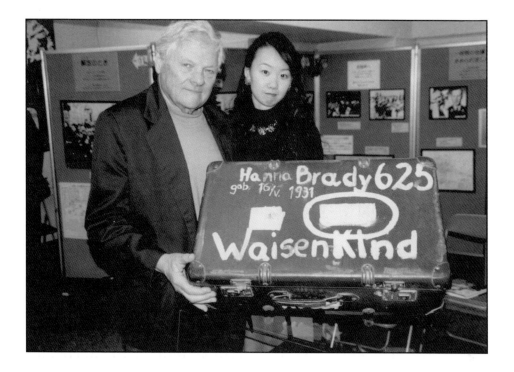

Acknowledgments

FIRST AND FOREMOST, my thanks go to George Brady and Fumiko Ishioka. This is their story. Each of them, with remarkable dedication and generosity, helped to bring the book together. They are very tenacious and compassionate people, driven by the desire to make the world a better place, and to bring attention and honor to the memory of Hana Brady. I salute them.

My heart jumped the first time I learned of Hana's suitcase in an article by Paul Lungen in the *Canadian Jewish News*. The story so touched me that I decided to come out of "exile" and produce my first radio documentary in a dozen years. The result was "Hana's Suitcase," which aired on *The Sunday Edition* on CBC Radio One in January 2001.

The first phone call I received after the broadcast came from a tearful Margie Wolfe, who said right then and there that I had to write this book. Margie is one of my favorite people in the whole world — a fiercely loyal friend and a hilarious, kooky, exuberantly talented woman whom I can now refer to as "my publisher" with feigned nonchalance.

Along with Margie, Sarah Swartz brought a clear and gentle touch to the editorial process. Jeffrey Canton, as well as the terrific women of Second Story Press — Melissa Kaita, Emma Rodgers, Phuong Truong, Kathryn Cole, and Carolyn Jackson — also made important contributions. Reynold Gonsalves knows that without his patience and skill in the radio studio and on the computer, my life would be much more complicated than it already is. Thank you also to Carmelita Tenerife for her sustaining care and Teresa Brady for her kindness.

My sensational women friends were morale boosters, babysitters, and all-around hand holders in this writing project: Susanne Boyce, Cate Cochran, Joy Crysdale, the late Brooke Forbes, Francine Pelletier, Geraldine Sherman, and Talin Vartanian.

No daughter could ask for more support and cheerleading from her parents. My mother, Helen, and my late father, Gil, taught me (among many other things) to celebrate human struggle, to know the past and to fight for a better future. And they gave me the best big sister, Ruthie Tamara, who has encouraged me in every way.

Michael Enright — my beau and covivant — thought I could write a book long before I did, and never missed an opportunity to tell me so. His confidence in me, and his unvarnished enthusiasm about this project, terrified and thrilled me at the same time. At every step, he gave me the nourishment I wanted, the prodding I needed, and the room to work. I am truly grateful for it all. I am also grateful for the trueheartedness of the Enright brood — Daniel, Anthony, and Nancy.

My beautiful son — Gabriel Zev Enright Levine — was six years old when the book was first published, too young to know Hana's story. He knows it very well now. Thanks to Hana, George, and Fumiko, he also knows that history matters, and that, sometimes, in the face of unspeakable evil, good people and good deeds can make a difference.

Hana's Suitcase

Play by
Emil Sher

Dedicated to my mother, Olga, a
Holocaust survivor who inspires through her
quiet commitment to an honest life.

Special thanks to Karen Levine, for
the gift of a book to behold, George Brady
and Fumiko Ishioka, who answered my questions
with grace and generosity, and to
Allen MacInnis for tilling the soil
so a play could flourish.

Hana's Suitcase

Hana's Suitcase was commissioned and developed by the Lorraine Kimsa Theatre for Young People (Artistic Director - Allen MacInnis; Managing Director - Nancy Webster). It was workshopped and received a public reading as part of the National Arts Centre's On the Verge New Play Reading Festival 2005.

Hana's Suitcase premiered at the Lorraine Kimsa Theatre for Young People in Toronto on March 9, 2006 with the following cast and creative team:

HANA BRADY	Jessica Greenberg
AKIRA	Richard Lee
MAIKO	Siu Ta
FUMIKO ISHIOKA	Jean Yoon
MARKETA BRADY/ LUDMILA/MICHAELA/ FRIEDL DICKER-BRANDEIS/ GRANDMOTHER	Sarah Orenstein
GEORGE BRADY	Paul Dunn
UNCLE LUDVIK/ KURT KOTOUC/VIKTOR ROTT	Doug MacLeod
KAREL BRADY/ GEORGE BRADY *(adult)*	Eric Trask
FIGURES *and others*	The Ensemble

Director	Allen MacInnis
Set and Costume Designer	Teresa Pryzbylski
Lighting Designer	Andrea Lundy
Composer	John Gzowski
Projection Coordinator	Daniele Guevara
Production Dramaturge	Nancy Guertin
Script Dramaturge	Stephen Colella
Stage Manager	Michael Sinclair
Assistant Stage Manager	Trina Sookhai

SETTING: Tokyo Holocaust Center, 2000 – 2001

PRODUCTION NOTE:

The play is punctuated with references to nameless Figures, ghost-like characters dressed in colorless clothing and full masks that reveal no emotions. The Figures are anonymous and have been stripped of details to reflect the casualties of war: victims are denied their identity as perpetrators lose their humanity.

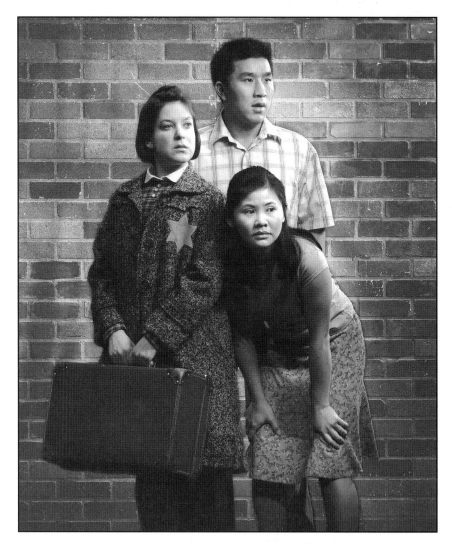

*Hana's Suitcase at Lorraine Kimsa Theatre for Young People
(Mar. 4-Apr. 23/06); clockwise from top: Richard Lee (Akira), Siu Ta
(Maiko) and Jessica Greenberg (Hana); Photo by Daniel Alexander*

Hana's Suitcase
Act 1

The lights slowly rise on Hana's suitcase, sitting on a table. Akira steps forward. He looks to see if he's being watched, then checks again for good measure. Slowly, carefully, he unlocks the suitcase. He hesitates, then slowly opens it.

Hana enters on her scooter, ghost-like, circling the stage. Akira is unaware her spirit is there. He peers into the suitcase. Maiko enters.

MAIKO: Akira!

Akira immediately closes the suitcase.
Hana exits.

MAIKO: What are you doing?

AKIRA: Nothing.

MAIKO: You opened the suitcase.

AKIRA: There might be something inside.

MAIKO: It's empty.

AKIRA: Something hidden.

MAIKO: We checked.

AKIRA: We can check again.

Akira makes a move to open the suitcase again.

MAIKO: Akira! You're not supposed to open it. You heard what Ms. Ishioka said. You must treat the suitcase like you would treat your own grandmother.

AKIRA: I love my grandmother.

MAIKO: Then treat the suitcase the same way. With care and respect.

AKIRA: My grandmother doesn't have a name painted on her. My grandmother —

MAIKO: — won't live forever. Who will remember her when she's gone?

AKIRA: Me.

MAIKO: Who remembers Hana?

AKIRA: *(Pause)* Is Hana gone?

MAIKO: I don't know. Her suitcase may be all that's left. That's why you must treat it with respect.

AKIRA: She was an orphan. A *Waisenkind.* That's what it says on her suitcase. *Waisenkind.*

MAIKO: I can read.

AKIRA: You can't read German. *(Beat)* Was she German?

MAIKO: You ask too many questions.

AKIRA: You don't know.

MAIKO: I know she was born on May 16, 1931.

AKIRA: You don't know where.

MAIKO: I know she was in Auschwitz.

AKIRA: You don't know when.

MAIKO:	I know she was an orphan.
AKIRA:	*(Pause)* You don't know what kind.
MAIKO:	An orphan is an orphan, Akira.
AKIRA:	We don't know when she became an orphan. You can become an orphan when you're still a baby, or when you're a big kid. *(Beat)* Was Hana a baby orphan or a big kid orphan?

Akira reads Maiko's face.

	You don't know. You don't know anything about Hana.
MAIKO:	I know I don't want to be an orphan.

Fumiko enters.

FUMIKO:	You sound like two birds fighting over a crumb.
AKIRA:	I want to know more about Hana Brady.
MAIKO:	So do I.
AKIRA:	All we have is her suitcase. *(Beat)* An empty suitcase.
FUMIKO:	The museum also sent us a sock, a shoe and a sweater.
MAIKO:	And the container of Zyklon B.
FUMIKO:	All of it can be shown in our exhibition.
AKIRA:	It's not Hana's sock. Or her sweater or shoe. They didn't belong to Hana.
FUMIKO:	They belonged to children just like Hana Brady.
MAIKO:	Gas. *(Low)* That's how many of them died. They were gassed.
FUMIKO:	*(Pause)* Yes.

MAIKO: That's what the Zyklon B was for.

FUMIKO: Yes.

MAIKO: One-and-a-half-million. That's what you told us. One-and-a-half-million children were killed.

Fumiko nods.

AKIRA: Was Hana the one?

FUMIKO: One what?

AKIRA: One child and half-a-million children. That's what you said. One, and a half-million. Was Hana the "One"?

MAIKO: It's not one child and half-a-million children. It's one million children, and then another half-a-million children.

AKIRA: Oh. *(Pause)* That means one-and-a-half-million suitcases.

FUMIKO: And we have one of them.

AKIRA: Her suitcase doesn't tell us anything.

FUMIKO: It gives us a name. Think of all the other children whose names we will never know.

AKIRA: I want to know more about Hana. What she packed in her suitcase. Where she took it. We don't know if she was tall. Or small. If she had long hair or short curls. If she had freckles or … or dimples. Did she wear bows in her hair, or colorful hats. *(Beat)* We don't know anything about Hana.

MAIKO: We know when she was born. And we know she was a *Waisenkind*.

FUMIKO: She wasn't always an orphan. She had parents. She had friends.

AKIRA: Maybe she had a dog. Or cats. Maybe she had cats and a dog. Maybe she had cats, a dog and a bird. Maybe she loved ice cream and … and hated asparagus, like me.

MAIKO: Maybe she loved the color green, like me.

FUMIKO: Maybe.

AKIRA: Can't we find out?

FUMIKO: It took a long time just to get Hana's suitcase.

AKIRA: Someone must know something about her.

MAIKO: *(Pause)* They're probably dead.

AKIRA: You don't know that.

MAIKO: The Holocaust wasn't a fairy tale.

AKIRA: I didn't say it was a fairy tale.

MAIKO: Most Jews who were sent to Auschwitz were killed in Auschwitz. They didn't live happily ever after.

Hana enters, holding her doll, Nana.

AKIRA: *(To Fumiko)* We don't know if Hana died at Auschwitz, do we? *(To Maiko)* We don't know if she was a baby orphan or a big kid orphan. We don't know if she loved chocolate or hated homework. We don't know if she liked to dance or draw or do cartwheels, because we don't know Hana's story.

Hana places the doll in her suitcase and exits.

FUMIKO: And if we did learn Hana's story and discovered it didn't have a happy ending. Would you still want to hear it?

AKIRA: Yes!

MAIKO:	I don't know.
AKIRA:	I'm not afraid of a story.
MAIKO:	Neither am I. But …
FUMIKO:	But what?
MAIKO:	Some stories are horrible. Really terrible.
AKIRA:	We don't know if Hana's story is horrible or terrible. We don't know if she lived in a big house with a small yard or a small house with a big yard. We don't if she walked to school or —
MAIKO:	Akira! *(Beat)* There's more to Hana's story than chocolate and cartwheels. You may not want to know all of Hana's story.
AKIRA:	I do. I want to know everything. Everything.
MAIKO:	So do I.
FUMIKO:	*(Pause)* I will find out all that I can about Hana.
AKIRA:	Yes!
FUMIKO:	But you must make me a promise.
AKIRA:	What kind?
FUMIKO:	We don't know where Hana's story will take us.
AKIRA:	What do you mean?
MAIKO:	She means Hana's story probably has a sad ending.
AKIRA:	I'm not afraid of sad endings.
FUMIKO:	If her story is a sad one, we must find a way out of the sadness. Agreed?
AKIRA:	Yes.

MAIKO: (*Beat*) Agreed.

AKIRA: How will you find out more about Hana?

FUMIKO: The same way we found her suitcase. I will write letters, asking for help.

AKIRA: To who?

FUMIKO: To Holocaust museums around the world. Maybe one of them can tell us something about Hana.

AKIRA: Someone must know her story.

MAIKO: Not always. Sometimes, when people die, their stories die, too.

AKIRA: Stories can't die.

FUMIKO: Stories can die if there is no one to tell them.

Hana appears, skipping on the spot.

Fumiko opens up a laptop and begins to compose a letter.

AKIRA: Who are you writing to?

FUMIKO: The Auschwitz Museum. They were kind enough to send us Hana's suitcase.

Music surfaces.

A museum official appears in a half-lit pool of light, stage right, face obscured by darkness. Names of individuals killed in the Holocaust appear on a scrim and disappear like mist.

OFFICIAL: We know nothing more about Hana Brady.

Hana stops skipping.

The light fades around the official and Hana.

FUMIKO: I will keep trying.

AKIRA: Who are you writing to?

Hana plays hopscotch.

FUMIKO: The Holocaust Memorial in Israel.

AKIRA: When will they answer?

MAIKO: Do you ever run out of questions?

AKIRA: No.

FUMIKO: We must be patient, Akira.

Music surfaces as more names appear and fade.

Half-light on another museum official, face lost in the shadows, stage left.

OFFICIAL: We have no record of Hana Brady.

The light around the second official fades.

Hana stops playing hopscotch. Fumiko perseveres.

MAIKO: Who are you writing to now?

FUMIKO: The Holocaust Museum in Washington.

AKIRA: Was Hana from America?

FUMIKO: No, Akira. Hitler invaded Europe.

AKIRA: When will Washington answer?

FUMIKO: We will hear from them soon, Akira.

More music, more names.

Hana appears, holding a birthday candle, eyes closed as she's about to make a wish.

A third museum official appears in a pool of light, centre stage, lost in the shadows.

OFFICIAL: We have no information about a Hana Brady.

The official is swallowed by the light. The music stops. Hana blows out the candle. The light around her goes out.

AKIRA: It's like she disappeared. Forever.

FUMIKO: We will find someone, Akira. Someone who can tell us more about Hana.

MAIKO: How?

FUMIKO: I don't know yet.

Lights fade to black.

The sound of a moving train slowly surfaces. Hana appears in the half-light, her suitcase by her side. She shares the cramped train car with four Figures, all with suitcases. They disappear as the light around them fades, but the sound of the train continues.

Lights up on Fumiko as she brandishes a letter.

FUMIKO: A letter! From the Auschwitz Museum. They found Hana Brady's name on a list.

AKIRA: What kind of list?

FUMIKO: A list that tells us Hana arrived at Auschwitz from a place called Theresienstadt, in the country that used to be Czechoslovakia.

AKIRA: Maybe she's a Czecher!

MAIKO: Was Hana born in The...res...ien...

FUMIKO: Theresienstadt. We don't know where she was born. But the more we learn about Theresienstadt, the more we will learn more about Hana.

AKIRA: I want to learn as much as we can.

FUMIKO:	Good. The next time we meet I want you to bring me some facts about Theresienstadt. For our exhibition.
AKIRA:	The Holocaust Seen Through Akira's Eyes.
MAIKO:	Through *Children's* Eyes.
AKIRA:	I'm a child.
MAIKO:	We know.
AKIRA:	What facts do you need?
FUMIKO:	I want you to find out about the children of Theresienstadt. When you come back to the centre next week I expect you to know more than you know today.
AKIRA:	We don't know anything today.
FUMIKO:	Then you will have a good week, Akira.

Fumiko exits. Maiko and Akira begin their research and share their findings.

MAIKO:	"Over the course of World War Two, more than 140,000 Jews were sent to Theresienstadt — 15,000 of them were children under the age of 15."
AKIRA:	Hana was one of the 15,000.
MAIKO:	Yes. But …
AKIRA:	But what?
MAIKO:	"Of those 15,000 children, fewer than 300 survived."
AKIRA:	Hana could be one of them.
MAIKO:	Chances are very low, Akira.
AKIRA:	I'm not afraid of low chances.
MAIKO:	I am.

AKIRA: Maybe Hana is still alive.

MAIKO: Most of the children who lived in Theresienstadt died in Auschwitz.

AKIRA: We don't know if Hana died. We don't know where she lived before she lived in Theresienstadt. Jews came to Theresienstadt from Denmark. And Poland. And Holland. That's why we have to keep digging. So we can find out where Hana was from. If we dig and dig and dig and dig and dig and —

MAIKO: All right, Akira.

Lights shift: a new day.

AKIRA: I'm confused.

MAIKO: You're young.

AKIRA: Did Hana live in Theresienstadt or Terezin?

MAIKO: "After the Nazis invaded Czechoslovakia, they turned Terezin into the Theresienstadt ghetto — a walled, overcrowded prison town to hold Jews who had been forced to leave their homes."

AKIRA: Why couldn't they stay where they were living?

MAIKO: This was a war, Akira. A terrible war.

AKIRA: Ms. Ishioka wants to know about Terezin when it was the Theresienstadt ghetto.

MAIKO: Then keep digging.

Lights shift: another day.

AKIRA: They had a garden.

MAIKO: I know.

AKIRA: Children worked in gardens, they grew fruits and
            vegetables and flowers.

MAIKO: All for the Nazi guards. While the guards ate fresh
            food, the inmates ate watery soup and black bread.

Lights shift: a new day.

            Look what I found.

Maiko opens her hand. Akira peers closely.

            Bugs!

Akira jumps back.

AKIRA: I don't see any bugs.

MAIKO: That's because you weren't there. Theresienstadt was
            full of bugs. Bugs in beds. Bugs in food. Bugs
            everywhere.

AKIRA: Fireflies.

MAIKO: All kinds of bugs.

AKIRA: Fireflies is the name of a fairy tale that some children
            performed. With music and dancing and singing.

MAIKO: Maybe they were trying to forget about the bugs.

Lights shift: another day.

AKIRA: They wrote their own newspaper, too.

MAIKO: Children or adults?

AKIRA: Children. *(Beat)* The Gong. The Madman.

MAIKO: Those must be nicknames.

AKIRA: They're poems. Poems by two of the boys who lived in
            Home Number One.

MAIKO: Home? I don't think so.

AKIRA: That's what it says.

MAIKO: That doesn't mean that's what it was.

AKIRA: They played a board game. Smelina. You moved your
            player from place to place around the board. The
            guards' barracks. The de-lousing station where they got
            rid of all the lice in the clothes.

MAIKO: Some game.

AKIRA: Players got to build a kumbal, an attic hideaway above
            the barracks.

MAIKO: The attics were their school.

AKIRA: They went to school?

MAIKO: Secret classes in secret attics.

Fumiko enters.

FUMIKO: You have done excellent work.

AKIRA: They had a secret school.

FUMIKO: I know. I've done some digging, too. The children were
            taught by an artist, Friedl Dicker-Brandeis. She hid
            some of the drawings by the children of Theresienstadt
            and they were found when the war ended.

AKIRA: Hidden drawings.

FUMIKO: Five thousand drawings.

MAIKO: Maybe some were by Hana.

AKIRA: Write to her! Maybe the art teacher knows Hana.

FUMIKO: Friedl Dicker-Brandeis was killed in Auschwitz.

AKIRA:	Oh.
FUMIKO:	But we can write to the Jewish Museum in Prague. That's where they keep the drawings that were found.
AKIRA:	Ask if they have any drawings by a girl named Hana Brady.
MAIKO:	We need some children's drawings. For the exhibition.
AKIRA:	The Holocaust Seen Through —
MAIKO:	Children's Eyes. Many children.
FUMIKO:	*(Pause)* I will try and find some drawings.
AKIRA:	Some of Hana's drawings.
FUMIKO:	I will try.
AKIRA:	What can we do?
FUMIKO:	Draw a picture of Hana.
AKIRA:	We don't know what she looks like.
FUMIKO:	Imagine what she looked like. Imagine what her life was like. Imagine what she drew in Theresienstadt.

Fumiko exits.

Akira and Maiko take their seats at a table. Hana joins them as if arriving at school, carrying her schoolbooks. She takes out a pencil and notebook and gets down to work. She raises her hand to answer questions, listens to her teacher, absorbs what's on the blackboard.

AKIRA:	Maybe she drew flowers.
MAIKO:	Or guards.
AKIRA:	Or rainbows.
MAIKO:	Or bread. Fresh bread and thick soup.

AKIRA: Was Hana with her family in Theresienstadt?

A school official appears in the shadows.

MAIKO: I don't know, Akira. *(Beat)* She was an orphan.

AKIRA: We don't know when she became an orphan. We don't know if she was a baby orphan or a —

MAIKO: Akira!

The official walks up to Hana's desk and takes away her textbook.

AKIRA: Why did the Nazis do that to the Jews?

MAIKO: You are asking too many questions.

AKIRA: What did the Jews ever do to them?

MAIKO: Nothing.

AKIRA: Nothing?

MAIKO: They were Jewish. That's all that mattered.

The official takes away Hana's notebook. Hana begins to write on her hand.

AKIRA: Have you ever seen one? A Jew.

MAIKO: No.

AKIRA: Me, neither.

MAIKO: When I do I will say, "I am very sorry for what happened to Hana."

AKIRA: We don't know what happened.

MAIKO: Ms. Ishioka will find out.

AKIRA: Then we'll know Hana's story.

The official takes away Hana's pen and exits.

MAIKO: *(Pause)* You and I will know Hana's story.

AKIRA: Yes.

MAIKO: What about Yuki?

AKIRA: Who is Yuki?

MAIKO: My cousin. She lives in Wakkanai. She never comes to Tokyo. She'll never see Hana's suitcase. Neither will Reiho. He moved to Abashiri.

AKIRA: We can send a picture of the suitcase.

MAIKO: It's not enough.

Hana exits.

AKIRA: Two pictures. A picture is worth a thousand words. Two pictures are worth two thousand words. Three pictures are worth —

MAIKO: Akira. *(Beat)* We'll use our own words.

AKIRA: No pictures?

MAIKO: Pictures and words. We'll share Hana's story with Yuki and Reiho in a newsletter.

AKIRA: We'll tell them about Hana's suitcase, and the sock, and the sweater.

MAIKO: And the poisonous gas.

AKIRA: And maybe some drawings from Theresienstadt.

MAIKO: We can make our own pictures, and poems, too.

AKIRA: I'm not a good poem maker.

MAIKO: Ikuno is a good poet. We can ask her to join us.

AKIRA: Saori, too.

MAIKO: Anyone who wants can help.

AKIRA: We will tell them everything we know. The more we
            know, the more we will tell. We will write to every child
            in every school. Every day.

MAIKO: Not every day.

AKIRA: Every week?

MAIKO: *(Beat)* Once a month.

AKIRA: We will call ourselves … Akira's Angels.

MAIKO: No. I will think of a name. You can draw a picture for
            our first newsletter. I will write about Theresienstadt.

Lights dim as Akira and Maiko begin their respective tasks.

Music.

Fumiko enters, holding a package.

FUMIKO: A package! From the Jewish Museum in Prague.

AKIRA: Hana's drawings!

MAIKO: Now we will see what she saw.

AKIRA: Maybe she drew a picture of herself.

MAIKO: A self-portrait.

AKIRA: We'll see what Hana looks like. Open it! Right away!
            (Beat) Right away, please.

Fumiko hesitates.

MAIKO: What's wrong?

FUMIKO: I don't know what to expect.

MAIKO: The drawings may be full of sadness.

Fumiko nods.

AKIRA: We will find our way out of the sadness.

FUMIKO: Yes. *(Pause)* Are you ready?

AKIRA and
MAIKO: Yes.

Fumiko slowly opens the package. She pulls out a cover letter and read.

MAIKO: What do they say?

Fumiko has trouble speaking.

FUMIKO: Hana's drawings. Pictures she drew in Theresienstadt.

Fumiko slowly pulls out the drawings from the package.

Screen: *Hana's drawings from Theresienstadt:*
           A garden and park bench
           A picnic by a river
           A tree
           Farmhands drying hay in a field
           Stick people carrying suitcases, getting off a train

AKIRA: She lived on a farm.

MAIKO: We don't know that.

AKIRA: Look. They're working on a farm.

MAIKO: That doesn't mean it's Hana's farm. Maybe she lived
           near a train station. See?

AKIRA: We don't know if it's the train station near her home.
           Maybe she rode a horse from her farm to get to the
           train station.

MAIKO: Maybe she took a train near her house and passed by a
           farm on her way to a picnic.

AKIRA: Maybe they made sandwiches for their picnic with cheese from the milk from the cows from their farm.

MAIKO: Maybe they —

FUMIKO: Maybe the cow made the sandwiches.

The sparring dissolves into grins.

             Let's get to work. Our exhibition is only a week away.

AKIRA: Do we have enough to show?

FUMIKO: We will start with a small exhibition.

AKIRA: I want a big exhibition.

FUMIKO: We will start with what we have.

AKIRA: Maybe there are more drawings by Hana.

Hana enters: she runs along a road but suddenly stops.

FUMIKO: Maybe.

MAIKO: Is there a museum in Terezin?

FUMIKO: Yes. The Terezin Ghetto Museum.

MAIKO: Maybe the Terezin Ghetto Museum knows something about Hana.

FUMIKO: I have written to them. *(Beat)* They had nothing more about Hana Brady.

Two Figures approach Hana. One is an inmate, crawling on his knees. The other is a guard, shoving the inmate forward with his foot.

AKIRA: That's what the other museum said, and they were wrong.

MAIKO: Which museum?

AKIRA: The other one. At Auschwitz. First they said they didn't have anything else about Hana Brady. Then they said they found her name on a list.

MAIKO: Museums make mistakes. Maybe the Terezin museum knows something about Hana but doesn't know it knows.

FUMIKO: Maybe.

AKIRA: Write to them again. Tell them museums make mistakes. Tell them to keep looking for something about Hana Brady.

Hana watches as the guard beats the inmate. She runs off.

MAIKO: We started with her suitcase. Now we have some of her drawings. *(Beat)* It's like the pieces of a puzzle.

AKIRA: I like puzzles. I want to know what Hana looks like. *(Beat)* Maybe she made a self-portrait.

The guard grabs the inmate by the scruff of the neck and drags him forward, offstage.

MAIKO: I want to know what happened to her.

AKIRA: The more we know about Hana, the more we can write in our newsletter.

FUMIKO: What newsletter?

AKIRA: We are going to write a newsletter. Me and Maiko and Ikuno and Saori. Every week.

MAIKO: Every month.

AKIRA: We will send it to every school.

MAIKO: Many schools.

AKIRA: In every country.

MAIKO: Just Japan.

FUMIKO: That's a wonderful idea.

MAIKO: We will call ourselves —

AKIRA: Akira's Angels!

MAIKO: Small Wings.

FUMIKO: Small Wings.

AKIRA: That's a good name. For now. *(Beat)* We need more pieces of the Hana puzzle.

FUMIKO: *(Pause)* I may be able to find more pieces.

MAIKO: How?

AKIRA: Where?

FUMIKO: I am going to London to speak at a conference. I could fly to Prague and travel to Terezin.

AKIRA: You will go to Terezin?

FUMIKO: *(Pause)* Yes.

Lights fade.

Music.

Lights up. Fumiko enters the empty corridors of the Terezin Ghetto Museum.

FUMIKO: Hello? *(Beat)* Hello? Is anybody here?

Silence. Fumiko ventures down the museum corridor until she reaches Ludmila's office.

LUDMILA: I am sorry. We are understaffed today. Please come back tomorrow.

FUMIKO: I cannot come back tomorrow.

LUDMILA: I have work to do.

FUMIKO: *(Beat)* I work for a museum, too. In Tokyo.

LUDMILA: I see.

FUMIKO: It is important I find out about a girl who once lived in Theresienstadt.

LUDMILA: Many children were in Theresienstadt.

FUMIKO: I want to find out about one of them. Hana Brady. We have her suitcase in our museum, and copies of drawings she made in Theresienstadt.

LUDMILA: *(Writing)* Hana Brady.

FUMIKO: You know her?

LUDMILA: I will give her name to my assistant when she comes to work tomorrow.

FUMIKO: I can't wait until tomorrow. I have to be back in Prague tonight.

LUDMILA: I don't have time. I'm by myself today.

FUMIKO: The work you do — *(Beat)* Children in Tokyo need to know about the children of Theresienstadt. Two children — Maiko and Akira — want to know about one child: Hana.

LUDMILA: Even if I helped you, I can't promise we will find anything about Hana Brady.

FUMIKO: I'm not sure how much I want to know.

LUDMILA: I don't understand.

FUMIKO: How much do you tell children about what happened? How much of the horror do you describe?

LUDMILA: I tell the children everything. Eventually. *(Beat)* Still, I have more questions than answers.

FUMIKO: For the children back home, Hana is the answer.

LUDMILA: *(Pause)* I will help you.

FUMIKO: Thank you …

LUDMILA: Ludmila.

FUMIKO: Thank you, Ludmila. I am Fumiko.

Three weak Figures, all inmates, approach. Each carries a large stack of books. The burden weighs them down: one is particularly weak.

Ludmila removes a book from one of the piles held by a Figure as if she had just pulled it off a shelf.

LUDMILA: These books hold the names of almost 90,000 men, women and children who were imprisoned at Theresienstadt and then sent to the east.

FUMIKO: To Auschwitz?

LUDMILA: Most went to Auschwitz.

FUMIKO: Where do we begin?

LUDMILA: One name at a time.

Sapped of all strength, the three Figures can barely withstand the burden of the books. Two Figures do their best to keep the middle Figure upright.

Music.

Ludmila and Fumiko carefully scan the lists.

A single name — an inmate at Theresienstadt — appears then fades on the screen. Another name appears, then fades. The names appear and fade, one at a time.

The middle Figure collapses. The other two Figures collect his books and add it to their piles, which they place on the ground. They drag the middle Figure off, too weak to lift his legs.

Hana enters, holding a buchta (doughnut), searching for George. She is in a different part of the camp and doesn't see the Figures.

Ludmila stops and looks up.

LUDMILA: Brady. Hana. May 16, 1931.

Fumiko reacts. Ludmila turns the book to show her Hana's name.

FUMIKO: How can I find out more about her?

LUDMILA: I don't know. This is all we have.

FUMIKO: *(Hesitant)* What does the check mark beside her name mean?

LUDMILA: *(Beat)* A check mark means they didn't survive.

Fumiko absorbs Ludmila's words.

LUDMILA: Like most of the 15,000 children at Theresienstadt she would have died at Auschwitz.

FUMIKO: I didn't think she had survived. *(Beat)* I will have to tell the children.

Fumiko and Ludmila honor the silence between them.

FUMIKO: This name here, on top of Hana's. Could this George Brady be her brother?

George enters.

LUDMILA: The Nazis tended to list families together. *(Beat)* George Brady was born in 1928. Hana Brady was born in 1931, in the same town.

Hana spots her brother and runs up to him.

FUMIKO: So she likely has a brother.

Hana and George embrace.

LUDMILA: Yes.

FUMIKO: There is no check mark beside George's name. He may still be alive. He would be able to tell us more about Hana.

Hana offers George her buchta but he refuses to take it. Hana persists.

LUDMILA: If he is still alive. If you found him. He could be living anywhere in the world. He could have changed his name.

FUMIKO: We could try to find out. We have nothing to lose.

LUDMILA: He might not want to talk about his past.

FUMIKO: I understand. But when he learns how much his sister means to the children, he might want to help.

George relents and takes the buchta. He kisses Hana. She runs off.

        Can you help me find George?

LUDMILA: When is your bus to Prague?

George runs off in the opposite direction from Hana.

FUMIKO: Two o'clock.

Ludmila takes two books and hands one to Fumiko.

FUMIKO: What am I looking for?

LUDMILA: Any reference to George Brady.

Fumiko and Ludmila begin to pore over names.

Screen: names of some of those who passed through Theresienstadt and died at Auschwitz, underscored with music.

Fumiko and Ludmila pore over the lists of names, turning page after page as the screen displays a flurry of names.

LUDMILA: Here!

FUMIKO: You found his name?

LUDMILA: Kinderheim L417. The Boys' House at Theresienstadt. George Brady is one of six boys listed together. Two boys would share a mattress on a bunk. Every bunk had three levels. There were forty-two boys in his room. *(Beat)* Oh!

FUMIKO: What?

LUDMILA: I know him.

FUMIKO: Who?!

LUDMILA: Kurt Kotouc. He shared a bunk with George Brady. *(Beat)* He is still alive.

FUMIKO: Where?!

LUDMILA: He used to work at the Czech National Art Gallery in Prague. I don't know how to get hold of him.

FUMIKO: I must try.

Ludmila writes an address on a sheet of paper that she hands to Fumiko.

The two remaining Figures return to collect the books. They lift them up and exit.

LUDMILA: Try the Jewish Museum in Prague. Ask for Michaela Hajek.

FUMIKO: I know Michaela Hajek. She sent me copies of Hana's drawings.

LUDMILA: Let's hope she can help again.

Fumiko embraces Ludmila.

FUMIKO: Thank you.

LUDMILA: You have a bus to catch.

One final embrace before Fumiko dashes off for her bus.

Blackout.

Fumiko approaches the doors of the Jewish Museum. She presses an intercom button. There is no reply. She presses the button again.

FUMIKO: Hello?

MUSEUM
GUARD: *(Through the intercom)* The museum is about to close for the day.

FUMIKO: I am here to see Michaela Hajek.

MUSEUM
GUARD: Come back tomorrow.

FUMIKO: I am leaving for Japan tomorrow. I must see Michaela.

MUSEUM
GUARD: Do you have an appointment?

FUMIKO: *(Pause)* She is expecting me.

Fumiko is buzzed through and enters the museum.

Lights up on Fumiko as she steps into Michaela's office.

MICHAELA: You must be Fumiko!

FUMIKO: Michaela?

MICHAELA: Ludmila told me to expect you. I'm so pleased to finally meet you.

FUMIKO: She told you about Kurt Kotouc?

MICHAELA: Yes. I've been trying to find him. They all say the same thing. "Have you tried this number?" or "Please leave a message." It will be very difficult to find Mr. Kotouc at this hour.

FUMIKO: If you can make a few more calls. I have been searching for months for something, anything I could find about Hana Brady. Now I know she had a brother, that her brother shared a bunk with Kurt Kotouc, that Kurt Kotouc lives in Prague. I want to give the children something when I go back to Tokyo. Something about George Brady.

MICHAELA: I will keep trying.

Music.

Michaela continues to make a series of phone calls.

Hana appears, desperately searching for her parents, wordlessly asking a succession of Figures (Theresienstadt inmates) if they have seen her mother or father.

Michaela finally makes the connection she's been searching for.

MICHAELA: I have reached his secretary!

Mikhaela hands the phone to Fumiko.

FUMIKO: This is Fumiko Ishioka. May I please speak to Mr. Kotouc?

He can't leave. Not tonight. Please. Not yet. I have to speak to him about George Brady.

I have to speak to him.

I will be on a plane soon. (*Beat*) I want to go back to Japan with an address. George Brady's address. Mr. Kotouc might have that address.

124

Can I speak to him on the phone?

Please. It is only one question: Do you know George Brady?

All I am asking for is one minute. One minute of his time.

I will come there. We can meet somewhere. Anywhere.

He was in Theresienstadt with George Brady. Hana Brady was there, too. She was killed. Mr. Kotouc survived. George … I don't know what happened to George Brady. Mr. Kotouc knows.

There are children in Japan who need to know what Mr. Kotouc knows. They need to know if Hana Brady had a brother who survived.

Hello? *(Beat)* Hello?! Are you still there?

All Fumiko hears is silence. She fears the worst.

Hana exits.

Thank you. Thank you, thank you, thank you.

Fumiko smiles at Michaela

He's coming here.

Her smile deflates.

What if Mr. Kotouc is coming to tell me
George Brady died?
What if he lost touch with George Brady?
What if he doesn't want to give me his address?
What if he doesn't have an address?
What if he decides not to come?

Lights up on Kurt Kotouc, who stands at the door of the office.

KURT: Who are you?

Fumiko turns around and faces Kurt Kotouc.

FUMIKO: My name is Fumiko Ishioka.

KURT: I know your name. But I don't know who you are.
            I don't know why you want to know about George
            Brady. My secretary said you spoke like your life
            depended on it.

FUMIKO: Not my life. Hana Brady's.

KURT: What do you know about Hana?

FUMIKO: We have her suitcase in our Holocaust Centre in Tokyo.

KURT: Her suitcase?

FUMIKO: And some of her drawings.

KURT: Where did you get Hana's drawings?

FUMIKO: It is a long story.

KURT: I want to hear it, but I don't have time.

FUMIKO: *(Pause)* Is George Brady …

KURT: He is alive.

FUMIKO: *(Beat)* He survived.

KURT: Why do you want to speak to George?

FUMIKO: He can tell us about Hana. About growing up with
            Hana. What they did as children. The games they
            played. The friends they made.

KURT: George and I are still friends. *(Beat)* You never forget the
            friends you made at Theresienstadt. He is alive and well
            and living in Canada.

FUMIKO: Where?

KURT: Toronto. In Toronto. He has three sons, and a daughter named Lara Hana. This is where you can reach George.

Kurt hands Fumiko a card.

FUMIKO: *(To herself)* I could call him.

KURT: It is best to write.

FUMIKO: Of course. I would not call him. But I could. I could pick up the phone and soon be speaking to George Brady. Hana Brady's brother.

KURT: Hana's suitcase. Hana's drawings. I don't know what he will say when you tell him.

FUMIKO: I don't know what I would say if I ever met him. *(Beat)* I can't thank you enough.

KURT: All this, for someone you never knew.

FUMIKO: I am getting to know her more and more.

KURT: I am still trying to understand you. Why you have done all that you have done.

FUMIKO: *(Beat)* For the children.

KURT: *(Pause)* For the children.

Kurt bows his head in appreciation, and exits.

MICHAELA: You are getting closer to Hana.

FUMIKO: Yes. I will write to her brother in Canada and hope for the best.

MICHAELA: The children in Tokyo will be so pleased.

FUMIKO: First, I must tell them what happened to Hana.

Blackout.

Sound: a train screeches to a halt. The train doors slide open with a terrifying clang.

Lights up on Hana and three Figures as they arrive at Auschwitz.

Sound: Barking dogs and guards yelling orders.

Hana and the Figures step forward, clutching their suitcases. Hana places her suitcase on the table at the Holocaust Centre in Tokyo, and exits.

Lights and sound fade.

Lights up. Akira and Maiko sit by Fumiko.

AKIRA: Is there a cemetery where she is buried?

FUMIKO: There is no cemetery at Auschwitz.

MAIKO: Auschwitz is a cemetery.

AKIRA: There is nothing left of Hana.

FUMIKO: That's not true, Akira. We have Hana's drawings. And her suitcase. And we still may learn Hana's story.

AKIRA: She's dead. Dead people can't talk.

FUMIKO: We must speak for those who are no longer here. *(Pause)* Not all the news I have is sad. *(Beat)* Hana Brady had a brother named George, and he survived.

MAIKO: Where is he?!

FUMIKO: In Canada.

AKIRA: Call him. Right away!

FUMIKO: A phone call from Japan, from someone he doesn't know, asking him about his sister. Imagine how he might feel.

AKIRA: Write him! Right away!

FUMIKO: I will send a letter to Canada tomorrow.

MAIKO: Can we send something with it?

FUMIKO: Of course. You and all the Small Wings.

MAIKO: I will write a poem.

AKIRA: I can't send a poem to George Brady. I try to make my poems rhyme but they never rhyme the way they're supposed to rhyme. By the time a word rhymes with another word it's too late, and George Brady will think, "This boy doesn't know how to write poems. None of the words —"

MAIKO: Akira!

FUMIKO: Draw a picture.

AKIRA: What kind?

FUMIKO: Any kind.

Akira and Maiko set down to create their works for George. Fumiko composes her letter.

FUMIKO: *Dear Mr. Brady, My name is Fumiko Ishioka, and I am the director of the Tokyo Holocaust Education Center. In July this year I met with Mr. Kurt Jiri Kotouc in Prague and I got your address from him. The reason why I am writing you is because we are now exhibiting your sister Hana Brady's suitcase at our Center. Please forgive me if my letter hurts you reminding you of your past difficult experiences. But I would very much appreciate if you could kindly spare some time to read this letter. Please let me start with a little explanation of what we do in Japan. The center aims at further promoting the understanding of the history of the Holocaust, especially among young children in this country. We believe it is our responsibility, too, to let our next generation learn the lessons of the Holocaust so that such a tragedy never be repeated again anywhere in the world. It is also very important for children, we believe, to think about what they can do to fight against racism and intolerance and to create peace by their own hands. The children here are all so excited to know Hana had a brother and he survived. I was wondering if you would kindly be able to tell us about you and Hana's story, the time you spent with Hana before you were sent to the camps, things that you talked about with her, you and her dreams, and anything that would help children here to feel close to you and Hana to understand what prejudice, intolerance and hatred did to young Jewish children. If possible, I would be grateful if you could lend us any kind of memorial items such as your family's photos. It will greatly help us further promote our goal to give every child in Japan a chance to learn about the Holocaust. I look forward to hearing from you.*

Fumiko exits.

Music surfaces.

Lights up at the Holocaust Centre.

AKIRA: Any letters from Canada?

MAIKO: Not yet, Akira.

AKIRA: Do you think George Brady will write back?

MAIKO: I hope so.

AKIRA: Do you think he liked my drawing of Hana?

MAIKO: I'm sure he did.

AKIRA: I bet he's glad I didn't send a poem.

MAIKO: I'm sure he loved everything we sent him.

AKIRA: But he may not answer.

MAIKO: No.

AKIRA: It might be too painful.

MAIKO: Yes.

AKIRA: He might be sick. Or blind. Or very, very weak.

MAIKO: We don't know, Akira. All we can do is wait.

George enters, sealing an envelope. Hana enters on her scooter. As George shows Hana the envelope she grins and grabs it while riding her scooter.

Fumiko enters, holding a package.

Hana exits. George runs after her.

FUMIKO: Akira! Maiko!

AKIRA: A package. From Canada.

MAIKO: What's inside?

Fumiko tears open the package. She pulls out a thick sheaf of pages and begins to read.

FUMIKO: It is here. *(Beat)* George Brady has given us Hana's story.

AKIRA: Is there anything else?

Fumiko peers into the envelope. She pulls out four photographs.

Screen: Pictures of Hana.

AKIRA: She's pretty.

MAIKO: She looks nice.

AKIRA: What did Hana's brother write about Hana?

FUMIKO: Listen …

Lights fade.

Hana and George

Hana's Suitcase
Act II

___

Winter. A dusting of snowflakes gently falls to the ground. Akira, Maiko and Fumiko watch in silent awe. The lights fade around them and rise on George.

George pretends to have found something on the ground.

GEORGE: Hana!

Hana enters and sees George has found something. Her curiosity is piqued. She approaches. George turns around and throws a snowball at her. Hana collects a snowball of her own and gives chase. They frolic through the backyard.

AKIRA: They made snowballs, too.

FUMIKO: They were children, just like you.

MAIKO: Please continue.

FUMIKO: "My mother had a big heart and a big laugh."

Marketa Brady steps into the yard.

MARKETA: Hana! George! It's time to go.

GEORGE: We're still playing.

MARKETA: You'll play at Uncle Ludvik's and Aunt Heda's. They're expecting us soon.

HANA: I want to go skating at the pond with Maria.

MARKETA: You'll see Maria at school. Sundays are for family.

HANA: Maria is like family.

MARKETA: Cousin Vera is even more like family. Go into the store
           and take a few of her favourite candies. And dress
           warmly for skiing.

FUMIKO: "My mother made sure that we always gave food to
           neighbors who were hungry."

AKIRA: If my parents owned a store I would eat candy all day.

FUMIKO: "My father used to call the cross-country ski races with
           a megaphone."

Karel Brady appears, holding a megaphone.

Akira and Maiko rejoin Fumiko.

*Marketa, George and Hana gather in a straight line, moving on cross-
country skis.*

KAREL: And the Brady family is off, spending another Sunday
           on skis. It looks like Marketa Brady is in the lead but
           George Brady is close behind. Hana Brady is not going to
           let her big brother get away with this. She'll not go down
           without a fight. What's this? Karel Brady is now joining
           the race. He must show everyone why he was proclaimed
           the champion skier in Nové Město na Moravě.

Karel takes his place at the front of the pack.

HANA: You're not the champion skier in Nové Město na
           Moravě.

KAREL: Not yet, Hanichka. It is only a matter of time.

*The rest of the family tries to keep up with Karel, who suddenly falls. He tum-
bles to the ground, sending everyone into a heap. They explode with laughter.*

Karel pulls a blanket from out of his knapsack. He shakes the blanket so that it lands on all four Bradys, who are now gathered on the parents' bed.

GEORGE: I love Sunday mornings.

HANA: I love snuggling in your bed.

A knock at the door punctures the tranquility.

MARKETA: We can't stay in bed forever.

HANA: A little longer?

Karel leaves to answer the door.

MARKETA: *(Smiling)* A little longer.

Marketa sings a lullaby/song. Everyone savors the Sunday morning ritual.

AKIRA: Who was at the door?!

MAIKO: Sshhh! Let Ms. Ishioka continue and we'll find out.

Karel returns to the family bedroom.

HANA: Who was at the door?

KAREL: A refugee.

AKIRA: What's a refugee?

KAREL: Someone who is forced to leave their home.

MAIKO: Why?

KAREL: *(To Hana)* Hitler is sticking his boots where they don't belong. First Austria. Now parts of Czechoslovakia. The man at the door wants nothing to do with the Nazis.

MARKETA: You gave him a little something, I hope.

KAREL: Of course. But there'll be others.

MARKETA: We'll feed them, too. That's no way to live. Fleeing their own homes.

HANA: Why can't they go back where they came from?

KAREL: It is getting difficult being a Jew.

HANA: What do you mean?

KAREL: It means neighbors are being fed lies about us. It means —

MARKETA: Karel!

Marketa leads Karel away and talks in low whispers.

Lights shift to signify a change in time.

FUMIKO: "At night, my parents would whisper, and Hana and I would wonder."

KAREL: Are they asleep?

MARKETA: Yes. They had a long day. Sundays are always so full.

KAREL: Viktor Rott is waiting for us in the living room.

MARKETA: Remind him to keep his voice down. I don't want him waking the children.

As soon as Karel and Marketa step away, Hana and George scamper out of the bed and position themselves so they can hear the adult discussion. Akira and Maiko do the same.

VIKTOR: We must all leave Nové Město na Moravě before it's too late. It's no longer safe for Jews to be here.

KAREL: Have you been threatened?

VIKTOR: Not yet, Karel. But it's just a matter of time. You can feel that war is in the air. We should leave Czechoslovakia for America, for Palestine, for Canada. Anywhere but here.

MARKETA: This is our home, Viktor. This is where we belong.

VIKTOR: The Jews of Germany said the same thing. And then there was Kristallnacht.

HANA: What's Kristallnacht?

Akira turns his head: he has just asked the question.

FUMIKO: It means The Night of Broken Glass.

GEORGE: A terrible night in Germany. The windows of Jewish stores were smashed.

FUMIKO: Synagogues were burned.

HANA: It couldn't happen here, could it?

Blackout.

Music surfaces.

The stage remains dark as Fumiko continues to read George's letter.

FUMIKO: "On March 15, 1939, the Nazis marched into the rest of Czechoslovakia and our lives were never the same again."

Lights go up halfway.

A movie theatre. Karel, Marketa, George and Hana squeeze by other moviegoers — Fumiko, Maiko and Akira — as they make their way to their seats. They reach their seats and sit down, back to the audience.

Screen: a black and white movie begins to play. The film lasts but for a minute before it stops. The screen goes blank.

The lights go up. The Bradys turn around, toward the audience, and look up at the projectionist's booth. They grumble aloud. Their backs are to the screen, where a stark message suddenly appears: JUDEN EINTRIT VERBOTEN.

AKIRA: What does that mean?

FUMIKO: "No Jews Allowed."

Marketa is the first to notice the sign. She tugs at Karel. Hana and George realize something is amiss. They turn and see the sign.

HANA: Why aren't we allowed to watch the movie?

KAREL: New rules, Hana.

GEORGE: New rules for Jews. Everyone else can stay and watch the movie.

MARKETA: Come, come. We'll have some sweets when we get back home.

HANA: I don't want to go home. I want to see the movie!

KAREL: We have to go.

AKIRA: *(To Fumiko)* It's not fair.

KAREL: I didn't say it was fair, Hana. I said we must go.

Marketa and Karel urge their children forward. Hana suddenly stops and waves.

GEORGE: Who are you waving at?

HANA: Maria.

GEORGE: *(Disgruntled)* Maybe she'll tell you what the movie is like.

HANA: Why isn't she waving back?

MARKETA: *(Beat)* She's afraid.

HANA: Of a movie?

MARKETA: Come, Hanichka.

They leave the theatre.

AKIRA: Why couldn't Jews watch movies?

FUMIKO: The Nazis wanted to make life more and more difficult for them.

MAIKO: What happened next?

George and Hana take their places at the family table.

FUMIKO: "It is hard to imagine, but things got worse."

Maiko and Akira find a place at the table.

Karel arrives at home and joins his family. He is visibly distraught. Marketa serves him his meal.

KAREL: I'm not hungry.

FUMIKO: "I'll never forget the look on my father's face that night."

MARKETA: What's wrong?

KAREL: It is getting harder and harder to be a Jew.

HANA: What happened to you?

KAREL: Not to me. To us.

GEORGE: What happened to us?

KAREL: From now on there is a curfew for all Jews.

HANA: What's a curfew?

FUMIKO: It means Jews are forbidden to be on the street after eight o'clock.

KAREL: We can only shop at certain stores.

MARKETA: That is ridiculous.

KAREL: It is the law.

GEORGE: Why are they so worried about a few Jewish families?

KAREL: We are the ones who must worry, Jirka.

George and Akira get up from their seats simultaneously.

KAREL: Wait!

FUMIKO: There is more.

KAREL: *(Pause)* Jews are forbidden to play in the park. *(Beat)*
            Jews are forbidden to play on the sports field.

HANA: That's not fair!

MAIKO: It's not right.

KAREL: I don't make the rules, Hana. *(Pause)* Jews are forbidden
            to skate on the pond.

HANA: I love to skate on the pond.

MARKETA: We know. We'll make do.

KAREL: There is more.

MARKETA: That is enough for one day. I want the children in bed
            early tonight. Tomorrow is a school day.

KAREL: *(Beat)* There is no school.

AKIRA: No school?

KAREL: Jews are forbidden to attend school.

HANA: Where ... Where will I go?

GEORGE: What will we do?

MARKETA: We will bring the teachers to you. To our house. We will
            hire tutors to teach you right in our home.

MAIKO: It's not the same.

HANA: I want to go to school with Maria.

GEORGE: Nothing is the same anymore.

Marketa consoles her children. Maiko and Akira step away. Lights shift.

FUMIKO: "The world around us was shrinking. Sometimes, at night, the stars were our only friends."

Marketa, Karel and Hana exit.

George steps into the backyard and falls to his knees. Hana enters, carrying a corked bottle.

HANA: Here's the bottle.

GEORGE: And here's the hole.

HANA: For what?

GEORGE: For the bottle.

George pulls out a pen and a pad of paper from his pocket.

HANA: I'm confused.

GEORGE: You're angry.

HANA: *(Pause)* I'm very angry.

GEORGE: Tell me one thing you are angry about.

HANA: I'm angry about many things.

GEORGE: Tell me one thing.

HANA: I can't skate with Maria at the pond.

George writes it down quickly, tears the sheet from the pad and stuffs it into the bottle.

HANA: What are you doing?

GEORGE: I'm going to stuff this bottle.

HANA: With paper?

GEORGE: It helps to write things down. You'll see. *(Beat)* Tell me something you're afraid of.

HANA: That we will become refugees like the people who have come to our door. That something will happen to Mommy and Daddy. *(Beat)* That someone will take you away.

George scribbles frantically, tears off the sheet, and stuffs it into the bottle.

HANA: *(Laughs)* Slow down.

GEORGE: I want to bury the bottle tonight. Before it gets too dark.

HANA: We can finish tomorrow.

GEORGE: Tonight. *(Beat)* Tell me something that makes you sad.

HANA: Maria and I were going to sing at school next month. Now I'll have to sing to myself. *(Beat)* What about you?

George scribbles it down and tears off the sheet.

GEORGE: You don't want me singing with you. I sound like a dog.

Hana takes the sheet and stuffs it into the bottle.

A wounded dog. (Beat) A wounded dog with a cold.

Hana smiles and takes the pen.

HANA: What makes you angry?

George grabs the pen back.

GEORGE: *(Grins)* I get angry when you take my pen.

HANA: I mean it.

GEORGE: You haven't finished yet. *(Beat)* Look up at the stars and
           make a wish.

Hana looks up at the sky, closes her eyes and makes a wish.

           What did you wish for?

HANA: I'm not telling.

GEORGE: I want to write it down.

HANA: If I tell you it won't come true.

GEORGE: Some wishes are for sharing.

HANA: *(Pause)* I wish we could be who we used to be.

George writes it down.

GEORGE: We're still the same.

HANA: Everything else is different.

GEORGE: Things will get better.

HANA: Do you think they will?

GEORGE: When this is all over, we'll dig up the bottle.

HANA: Yes.

GEORGE: We will read what we wrote and … and we'll laugh.

HANA: We'll laugh and drink lemonade. *(Beat)* Write this
           down: We need…

GEORGE: *(Writing)* We need …

HANA: … a bigger bottle.

GEORGE: … a bigger bottle.

HANA: This one …

GEORGE: This one …

HANA: … is much too small …

GEORGE: … is much too small …

HANA: … for a girl with hundreds and hundreds of wishes.

George stops writing and reads Hana's words. He slowly tears off the sheet and stuffs it into the bottle.

Hana grabs the pad and pen out of his hands.

HANA: Your turn. Make a wish.

George looks up.

GEORGE: *(Pause)* I wish wishes were enough.

Blackout.

The silence is fractured by a loud, insistent knock on a door that fills the theatre.

Lights up on Marketa. Karel, George and Hana sit downstage.

Akira and Maiko are by Fumiko's side.

FUMIKO: "In March 1941 my mother was arrested by the
           Gestapo."

AKIRA: What had she done?

FUMIKO: "My mother's brother had fled Czechoslovakia. She had
           been giving money to a man to send to her brother.
           That man kept a list. My mother's name was on his list.
           When he was arrested they found her name. She
           received a letter telling her to report to the Gestapo in
           Iglau the next morning."

AKIRA: For sending money to her brother?

FUMIKO: The Nazis didn't need an excuse to make life miserable for Jews. From Iglau, Marketa Brady was sent to Ravensbruck.

MAIKO: A concentration camp.

Marketa slowly walks toward her family.

FUMIKO: Yes.

AKIRA: Near Nové Město na Moravě?

FUMIKO: In Germany.

HANA: Germany? *(Beat)*

MARKETA: Just for now.

Hana cannot speak.

KAREL: We must all take care of each other while Mother is away.

GEORGE: When will you come back?

MARKETA: As soon as I can.

Karel stands nearby as Marketa embraces her children. She begins to rock them.

Akira takes a ball of clay and begins to mould it.

MAIKO: What are you doing?

AKIRA: My mother is leaving tomorrow. I am making a sun out of clay, so my mother will think of me every morning when she wakes up in Ravensbruck.

MAIKO: I will make a moon, so she will think of me at night.

AKIRA: *(To Fumiko)* You're Marketa.

MAIKO: What will you do?

FUMIKO: I will stay by my children's side for every moment they
            are awake.

MAIKO: And when they fall asleep?

*Marketa holds Hana and George in her arms. She rocks them, kisses them,
sings to them, strokes their hair. They fall asleep. She stands to leave.
Karel extends his hand. She squeezes it, then continues. Karel follows.*

FUMIKO: I will kiss them goodbye and try not to crumble like sand.

Lights fade to half.

Music.

Hana and George wake up and absorb the fact that their mother is gone.

Lights to full. Karel walks into the house, holding two packages.

KAREL: George! Hana! A package from Mother.

FUMIKO: "She had been gone for two months."

HANA: What's inside?

Karel opens one of the packages.

FUMIKO: "This was her first letter to us."

Karel shows the gifts Marketa has made.

KAREL: Look!

FUMIKO: "And her last."

GEORGE: Hearts made of bread. And a horseshoe, too.

HANA: With our initials.

KAREL: And a heart for cousin Vera, too.

FUMIKO: "Instead of eating the bread herself she made it into
            gifts for us."

HANA: What does the letter say?

KAREL: It's to you.

HANA: "My dearest one, I wish you all the best on your
          birthday. I am sorry that I can't help you blow out the
          candles this year. But the heart is a charm I made for
          your bracelet. Are your clothes getting too small for
          you? Ask Daddy and Georgie to speak to your aunts
          about having some new ones made for my big girl.

HANA and
FUMIKO: "I think about you and your brother all the time. I am
          well. Are you being a good girl? Will you write me a
          letter? I hope you and George are keeping up your studies.

FUMIKO: "I am well. I miss you so much, dearest Hanichka. I am
          kissing you now. Love, Mother. May 1941. Ravensbruck."

HANA: I want to show Maria my beautiful heart.

Hana gets up to leave.

KAREL: Wait!

Karel's tone startles Hana.

          You can't leave the house.

HANA: It's not curfew yet.

KAREL: There are new rules.

GEORGE: We can't leave the house?

KAREL: We can leave but we need to wear these when we step
          outside.

*Karel pulls out three squares of yellow cloth from the second package and
hands them to Hana and George.*

HANA: Why?

GEORGE: Everyone knows we're Jewish.

KAREL: We have no choice. Cut out the star and pin it to your coat.

HANA: I'll show Maria my heart another time.

Hana walks off. George follows.

Akira and Maiko watch as Karel takes a pair of scissors and cuts out his star.

AKIRA: I wouldn't wear one.

MAIKO: Everyone had to.

AKIRA: What if I didn't? They've already said no more school, no more skating at the pond.

MAIKO: No more swinging at the park.

AKIRA: What else could they do?

FUMIKO: They could punish you, Akira.

AKIRA: I'm not afraid of punishments.

FUMIKO: You've never been punished like this.

MAIKO: Like how?

FUMIKO: "One day in September 1941, one of the Jewish men in Nové Město na Moravě decided he had had enough of all the rules and regulations. Instead of cutting out the Star of David as he was told to do, he pinned the entire cloth to his coat. This made the Nazi official in charge of Nové Město na Moravě very angry."

AKIRA: How angry?

Fumiko hesitates.

MAIKO: What happened?

FUMIKO: The Nazi official declared that Nové Město na Moravě must be made judenfrei, free of Jews, right away.

AKIRA: Free of Jews?

MAIKO: All Jews?

A knock on the Bradys' door. Karel exits.

FUMIKO: All the men.

George and Hana enter and see their father being taken away.

Hana screams. George holds her back from running after Karel. She collapses in his arms.

GEORGE: I will take care of you.

HANA: And who will take care of you?

GEORGE: We have each other.

HANA: *(Pause)* What if they take you away?

GEORGE: I'm not going anywhere.

Another knock. George goes to answer the door.

HANA: George, no!

Another knock.

GEORGE: If we don't open it, they'll knock it down.

George walks toward the front door.

LUDVIK: *(Offstage)* George? Hana?

Ludvik enters.

HANA: Uncle Ludvik!

Hana runs to embrace him.

AKIRA: *(To Fumiko)* You said they took away all the Jewish fathers.

FUMIKO: Uncle Ludvik was married to Karel's sister, Heda.

LUDVIK: I got here as soon as I heard the bad news.

FUMIKO: He was Christian and so he was spared.

HANA: What are we going to do?

LUDVIK: You are both coming with me. Aunt Heda and I will take care of you until your parents return.

HANA: When are they coming back?

LUDVIK: I don't know, Hanichka.

HANA: We should be here when they get back.

LUDVIK: If they see you are not here they will know where to look.

GEORGE: What should we take with us?

LUDVIK: Take what is most important to you.

Hana and George head to their bedroom.

             Vera will be so happy to see you.

Ludvik steps out.

Hana and George return a moment later with an armful of clothing and luggage to put it in. Hana carries her unmarked suitcase.

AKIRA: She took her suitcase!

They begin to pack.

FUMIKO: They spent the winter with their uncle, aunt and cousin.

HANA: What special thing are you going to take?

George holds up a photo album.

GEORGE: All our family photographs. What are you bringing?

Hana dashes off.

GEORGE: Hana!

She returns with her beloved doll.

        Hana and Nana.

Hana places the doll in her suitcase. Hana and George exit.

Akira cavorts around the centre as if he was a superhero.

MAIKO: What are you doing?

AKIRA: I am The Avenger. I will save my nephew and niece.
           I will protect them.

Akira performs a series of karate kicks and other superhero maneuvers.

FUMIKO: Akira.

AKIRA: I will eradicate evil.

FUMIKO: Akira!

Akira stops.

FUMIKO: Do you know what "avenger" means?

AKIRA: I know it's a good name for a superhero.

MAIKO: It's when you take revenge.

AKIRA: "Eradicate" is like … like erasing.

Akira launches into a short-lived assault.

FUMIKO: Uncle Ludvik was a different kind of hero. He risked his
           life taking Hana and George into his home.

MAIKO: But he was not superhuman.

FUMIKO: Listen. "Uncle Ludvik's house was small but
            comfortable. We spent time with our cousin Vera but
            could not go to school with her. We lived there from the
            fall of 1941 until the next spring."

MAIKO: And then?

FUMIKO: "One day, our aunt and uncle received a notice. We
            were ordered to report to a deportation centre at Trebic,
            near Nové Město na Moravě, on May 14, 1942."

*Hana and George enter, carrying their suitcases for the trip to Trebic.
George holds his photo album. Hana clutches her doll.*

Ludvik enters.

LUDVIK: Think of it as a trip.

HANA: I don't want to go.

LUDVIK: At least you'll be together. You'll be going to a place
            with lots of children. Jewish children. Maybe you won't
            have to wear the star.

HANA: Will my parents be there for my birthday?

LUDVIK: I don't know, Hana.

GEORGE: Who will take us to Trebic?

LUDVIK: I have arranged for my brother to take you. By horse
            and train.

HANA: You can't come?

LUDVIK: It's too – *(Pause)* Aunt Heda and I want to say goodbye
            to you from here. This is where we will say goodbye.
            This is where we will see you when the war is over.
            (Pause) Yes.

Hana gives her doll to her uncle. George hands him the photo album. They embrace. Ludvik exits.

FUMIKO: "We were taken to a warehouse in Trebic. There were very few children. There were hundreds of Jewish women and men, waiting to be deported to Theresienstadt."

AKIRA: Theresienstadt!

George fishes a small candle and a few candies from his suitcase.

GEORGE: I brought a few candies from home. And a candle.

George lights the candle.

GEORGE: Happy Birthday.

He gives his sister a kiss.

MAIKO: She was only eleven years old.

GEORGE: Make a wish.

Hana closes her eyes. Marketa and Karel appear on stage and take their place, dream-like, beside Hana. She smiles, and blows out the candle.

Blackout.

Sound: A guard's whistle.

VOICE: Everyone is to appear at the train tracks in one hour. Each person is allowed one suitcase. Form straight lines. No talking. Do as you are told.

Sound: A train door is slammed shut. The train clangs along the tracks.

Lights up. Hana and George sway to the rhythm of the train, squeezed between three Figures.

HANA: Maybe Mommy and Daddy are at Theresienstadt.

GEORGE: Maybe.

FUMIKO: They would have felt like sardines in that train. *(Beat)* There would have been crying, too. You would have smelled the fear.

AKIRA: I don't smell things when I'm afraid.

FUMIKO: You have never been on a cramped train, heading to a camp like Theresienstadt.

AKIRA: They didn't know what Theresienstadt was like.

MAIKO: That's why they were so afraid.

Sound: The train stops. The doors open.

Hana and George begin to walk. Akira and Maiko follow them, as if they were part of the procession.

FUMIKO: "When we reached the fortress we saw that the boys and men were going in one direction and the girls and women were being sent in another."

HANA: Where are they going?

GEORGE: I don't know.

HANA: Can I stay with you?

GEORGE: Sssh! We mustn't draw attention to ourselves.

GUARD'S
VOICE: Open your bags.

AKIRA: What was he looking for?

FUMIKO: Money and jewellery.

VOICE: Where are your parents?

GEORGE: They are in another camp. We are hoping to meet them here.

GUARD: *(To George)* To the left! *(To Hana)* To the right!

MAIKO: No!

HANA: Please, I beg you. Can I stay with my brother?

GUARD: Move! Now!

George gives Hana a quick hug.

GEORGE: Don't worry. I'll find you as soon as I can.

Hana watches George walk away. She picks up her suitcase and walks off in the other direction. Both walk offstage.

AKIRA: Where did she go?

FUMIKO: Kinderheim L410. A large barrack for girls. That was Hana's home for the next two years.

AKIRA: Kinderheim?

FUMIKO: It means "children's home."

MAIKO: It couldn't have been much of a home.

FUMIKO: There was never enough room, never enough food, never a chance for a private moment. There were too many people, too many bugs and rats, too many rules. Everyone in Theresienstadt tried to make the best of a terrible situation.

Hana enters.

AKIRA: How?

MAIKO: Remember? They met secretly to study.

FUMIKO: "There were secret classes held in the attic of Hana's barracks. At the end of each class, one child was chosen to sing a favorite song from back home."

Hana proudly takes her place at the front of her class. She sings softly.

HANA: Stonozka (The Centipede Song)
            Her life is not a piece of cake.
            Imagine how she suffers when
            She walks until her tootsies ache.
            She's got good reason to complain.
            So when I want to cry the blues
            I just recall the centipede.
            Consider walking in her shoes
            And then my life seems sweet indeed.

AKIRA: Why did they have to sing softly?

MAIKO: *(Short)* So the guards wouldn't hear.

AKIRA: *(Defensive)* I wasn't there, okay.

MAIKO: What other classes did Hana have?

FUMIKO: *(Scans George's letter)* Sewing.

AKIRA: And art. We have some of her drawings.

FUMIKO: *(Nods)* Remember? Hana had a famous painter for her teacher.

AKIRA: Picasso? I did a project on Picasso.

FUMIKO: No, not Picasso. Friedl Dicker-Brandeis.

Friedl Dicker-Brandeis appears. Hana takes her seat. Akira and Maiko sit down beside her.

HANA: What should we draw?

FRIEDL: We can begin by drawing the world around us. Don't be afraid to draw what you see.

MAIKO: *(To Fumiko)* Like what?

HANA: Like people waiting in line for food?

FRIEDL: *(Beat)* Yes.

HANA: Yesterday …

FRIEDL: Yes?

HANA: *(Pause)* Yesterday I saw …

FRIEDL: Draw what you saw.

Lights up on two Figures in a frozen moment: a guard kicking a prisoner crawling on the ground.

FRIEDL: Sometimes, it helps to put our sadness down on paper.

Hana continues to sketch.

AKIRA: Not all of Hana's pictures were sad. Remember the one of the picnic?

FUMIKO: Of course. More than anything, Friedl Dicker-Brandeis wanted the children to use art to make their lives better.

MAIKO: How?

FRIEDL: Think of space.

HANA: What kind of space?

FRIEDL: The space that isn't here. The space you want and need. Space to run around in. Space to jump through. Space where your imagination can run wild.

HANA: I want to go back to Nové Město na Moravě.

FRIEDL: Go back using your pencil and paper.

HANA: Past the ghetto walls?

FRIEDL: Wherever you want to go. Think of freedom.

HANA: The freedom to be with my parents and brother again?

FRIEDL: Show me what is in your hearts. All of you. Put it down on paper.

HANA: No one will ever see the drawings we've made.

FRIEDL: *(Pause)* What counts is that you have made them.

Music.

Screen: Selected drawings by children at Theresienstadt.

The drawings fade.

FUMIKO: "At first we could only meet for two hours a week. And for the first weeks we kept missing each other."

Hana runs up to a Figure.

HANA: George? George Brady? Have you seen him?

The Figure shakes his head.

Hana spots George and runs up to him. They embrace.

HANA: I'm so happy to see you!

GEORGE: I have thought of you every day, Hana.

HANA: Have you heard anything about Mommy and Daddy?

GEORGE: Not yet. But who knows? They could show up any day, and we'll all be together again.

HANA: That is the dream I dream all day and all night.

GEORGE: Are you getting enough to eat?

HANA: No. I'm always hungry.

GEORGE: We must try and stay strong.

HANA: It's hard when there's so many of us here and so little food.

GEORGE: We must do our best.

George shows Hana his wrench.

HANA: What's that?

GEORGE: I'm learning to be a plumber.

HANA: A plumber! I never would have imagined it.

GEORGE: Do you still want to be a teacher?

HANA: *(Nods)* One day, I will stand in front of a classroom and all the students will call me Miss Brady.

GEORGE: I will sit at the back of your classroom and make rude noises.

Hana hits George playfully. George lifts Hana as he hugs her.

HANA: Careful! You'll squish my buchta.

George releases her. Hana takes a small doughnut out of her pocket.

I saved this for you.

GEORGE: It's your buchta, Hana. It's too special to share.

HANA: I'm not sharing it with you. *(Grins)* I want you to have it all.

She hands it to George.

Bigger brothers have bigger stomachs.

GEORGE: Thank you.

HANA: I will give you my next buchta, and the next and the next and the next.

GEORGE: Do you want me to turn into a buchta?

HANA: *(Beat)* I want to go back home with you. I want to see Mommy and Daddy again.

George nods and takes Hana into his arms once more.

FUMIKO: "As the days and months passed, Theresienstadt
            became more crowded and cramped. The weak became
            weaker. The sick became sicker. And Hana never gave
            up looking for any scrap of information she could find
            about our parents."

Hana runs up to three Figures.

HANA: Do you know Karel and Marketa Brady? Have you ever
            been to Ravensbruck? My mother is there. Maybe you
            have seen her.

They all shake their heads.

FUMIKO: Hana and George did see a familiar face in
            Theresienstadt.

AKIRA and
MAIKO: Who?

FUMIKO: Their grandmother.

HANA: She is here?!

GEORGE: She arrived last night.

*Light up on their grandmother, lying on the floor, her hair disheveled and
her clothes soiled and torn.*

FUMIKO: "We found her in an overcrowded attic."

Hana and George approach their grandmother.

HANA: Babichka, it's me. Hanichka.

Hana's grandmother barely has the strength to lift her head.

HANA: I brought you a drawing I made.

Hana unrolls the drawing but her grandmother is in no condition to look at it.

GEORGE: *(Low)* She doesn't look well, Hana.

HANA: She should be back in her apartment in Prague.

GEORGE: Giving us bananas and oranges.

HANA: *(Beat)* We never thanked her for the scooters she gave us.

GEORGE: We did. We sent a card.

HANA: I wish I could thank her again. Back home.

GEORGE: She's so weak.

HANA: No wonder. It's like an oven in here.

Hana folds her drawing into a fan and begins to cool her grandmother. She hums a song. George joins her.

FUMIKO: Old people were given the smallest and worst rations. What little food they were given was crawling with bugs.

GEORGE: Things will get better, Hana.

HANA: Mommy and Daddy are counting on us to stay strong.

Hana slowly stops fanning. The humming fades.

FUMIKO: "Three months after she arrived at Theresienstadt, our grandmother was dead. No one really noticed."

The light around their grandmother fades to black. Hana and George walk away.

Akira walks off.

MAIKO: Akira!

He keeps walking.

MAIKO: Akira!

Maiko grabs a hold of him.

MAIKO: Where are you going?

AKIRA: I want to go home.

MAIKO: We made a promise.

FUMIKO: I haven't finished George Brady's letter.

AKIRA: I don't want to hear any more.

FUMIKO: We should listen to all of Hana's story.

AKIRA: Why?

MAIKO: So we can share it. The Small Wings must share Hana's story.

AKIRA: Why?

FUMIKO: So children will think exactly what you are thinking.

MAIKO: That what happened to Hana wasn't fair.

MIKO: Yes. And that what happened to Hana should never have happened.

AKIRA: How can we make it not happen again?

FUMIKO: *(Pause)* I don't know what makes people do what they do. But I believe, Akira, that when you open hearts, you open up minds. *(Beat)* A closed mind is a dead end.

AKIRA: A dead end is a dead end because something blocks you at the end.

MAIKO: Like a wall.

AKIRA: Or a fence.

MAIKO: Or a river.

AKIRA: Or a field.

FUMIKO: I didn't say it was easy.

AKIRA: *(Pause)* You can climb over the wall. Or … or swim across the river. Then it's not a dead end anymore even though the sign says "Dead End." They can change the sign so it says "Not really a dead end if you don't mind climbing a wall or swimming across a river."

FUMIKO: How will you get over the wall at the end of a closed mind?

MAIKO: *(Pause)* We can make a book. A book about Hana's life.

AKIRA: A book will take too long.

FUMIKO: A poem.

AKIRA: A poem's too hard.

MAIKO: A song.

AKIRA: A song's too short.

Akira ponders the possibilities.

            Beni.

MAIKO: Who?

AKIRA: Beni the talking Bed. When I was in Grade One I saw a play in school. About a boy who … who was afraid of monsters under his bed. And the bed could talk. And Beni the bed told the boy things I never forgot. *(Beat)* We can go from school to school to school and put on a play about Hana's suitcase. A … A suitcase that talks.

MAIKO:	We can do the talking.
AKIRA:	I can be George.
MAIKO:	I can be Hana.
AKIRA:	*(To Fumiko)* You can be everyone else.
MAIKO:	The Small Wings can perform the play. Ikuno can be Marketa.
AKIRA:	Nobuo can be Karel.
MAIKO:	Aya can be Friedl the art teacher.
AKIRA:	And I will be famous!
FUMIKO:	Don't do it to be famous, Akira.
AKIRA:	I will do it for Hana. *(Beat)* I am ready to write the Hana play.
FUMIKO:	You haven't heard the rest of Hana's story.
AKIRA:	*(Pause)* I am ready to hear the rest of Hana's story.
FUMIKO:	"By September, 1944, when the Nazis began to realize that they were losing the war they announced that more people would be leaving Theresienstadt."
AKIRA:	They let them go?
MAIKO:	No, Akira. Trains took the Jews of Theresienstadt to Auschwitz.
FUMIKO:	"Dreaded lists would be posted in each building. People whose names were on the list had to report to an assembly hall close to the railway station within two days."

Lights up on Hana, scanning a list. Her finger stops at a name.

She stumbles toward George, who has been waiting for her.

They embrace.

HANA: What will I do without you here?

GEORGE: You must eat as much as you can, Hana. You must take care of your health and be as strong as you can be.

HANA: I don't feel very strong right now.

GEORGE: I promised Mother and Father that I would take care of you so we can all be a family again. I don't want to break that promise, so I need your help. You must be as strong as you can until we see each other again.

Hana nods.

Sound: Curfew whistle.

GEORGE: We must go back to our barracks.

Hana hugs George with all her might. They separate. George runs off. Hana stands in a pool of light.

FUMIKO: "After the war, I returned to Nové Město na Moravě and searched for Hana. One day in Prague I met a young woman who had lived with Hana in Theresienstadt. She told me what had happened to my young and beautiful sister. *(Beat)* I try to imagine what Hana's last days were like. I wish I could have been there to protect her."

Friedl approaches Hana.

FRIEDL: I am being taken away, Hana.

HANA: You, too?

FRIEDL: Some day soon it may be your turn. You must look your best.

HANA: I promised George I would look healthy.

Friedl uses a small rag to keep Hana's hair in a ponytail.

FRIEDL: There. *(Beat)* Remember to pinch your cheeks.

Friedl pinches Hana's cheeks to give them color.

HANA: Remember to pinch yours.

Hana gently pinches Friedl's cheeks.

You look beautiful.

FRIEDL: I don't feel beautiful right now.

HANA: You don't see what I see. That's what you taught us. To see things not everyone else sees. I will always see things differently, because of you.

FRIEDL: Thank you.

Friedl kisses Hana and leaves.

FUMIKO: "Four weeks after I was taken to Auschwitz Hana found her name on a list."

Hana pinches her cheeks, steps forward and picks up her suitcase.

Sound: Barking dogs, yelling guards.

Hana steps onto a cramped train, between two Figures who share the same fate.

Sound: The train doors are slammed shut. The train begins to roll away. Everyone sways.

MAIKO: I would hate not knowing where I was going.

AKIRA: They're going "east."

MAIKO: East is Auschwitz, Akira. Hana didn't know what to expect.

AKIRA: She was expecting to see George.

FUMIKO: The train chugged for a day and a night. There was no food. No water. No toilet. Just a bucket.

AKIRA: What was Hana thinking as the train went east?

MAIKO: She must have been very afraid.

FUMIKO: Yes.

AKIRA: Very lonely.

FUMIKO: Yes.

The train screeches to a halt. Blackout.

Lights up. Fumiko, Akira and Maiko watch from a distance as Hana steps off the train, into a pool of searchlights. She is followed by the two Figures.

Sound: Barking dogs.

GUARD: *(Voice only)* You! Over there, to the right!

Hana looks at the Figure who has been chosen.

GUARD: You, too.

Hana sees the guard is talking to the second Figure.

AKIRA: Where were they taking them?

FUMIKO: The strong ones were used for slave labor.

GUARD: The rest of you, step forward.

Hana, holding her suitcase, steps forward.

AKIRA: And the rest?

GUARD: Leave your suitcases on the platform.

Hana places her suitcase down.

FUMIKO: If you were weak or old or a child, they wasted no time. You were sent to your death.

GUARD: Follow the guard.

MAIKO: Gas. They used gas.

AKIRA: All the children?

FUMIKO: Most.

GUARD: Move!

Hana walks upstage, along a corridor of light. When she reaches the end of the corridor she stops.

The corridor of light shrinks so all that's left is Hana, standing in a pool of light. As the light around her fades, the light around her suitcase grows. Soon, the suitcase is fully lit, and Hana is gone.

Akira walks over to the suitcase. He turns it around and reveals the writing on it: Hana Brady. 16/V. Waisenkind.

AKIRA: Do you think George Brady will like our play?

FUMIKO: I'm sure he will.

Fumiko exits.

AKIRA: When is he going to get here?

MAIKO: Very soon.

AKIRA: Will George Brady mind that I'm pretending to be George Brady?

MAIKO: No.

AKIRA: I'm not Jewish.

MAIKO: That doesn't matter.

AKIRA: Why won't he mind?

MAIKO: You and me and all the other Small Wings are telling Hana's story.

AKIRA: And that will make him happy?

MAIKO: I think so.

AKIRA: Do you think he misses Hana?

MAIKO: Yes.

AKIRA: Even after all this time?

MAIKO: Yes.

AKIRA: I miss her, too. *(Beat)* Do you know what I mean?

MAIKO: *(Beat)* Yes.

Fumiko enters. With her is George Brady as he is today. Akira and Maiko are speechless.

FUMIKO: This is Akira.

GEORGE: Akira.

Akira places a garland of origami paper cranes around his neck. He bows. George returns the gesture.

FUMIKO: This is Maiko.

GEORGE: Maiko.

Maiko bows. George does the same.

FUMIKO: This is your sister's suitcase.

George stares at the suitcase.

FUMIKO: The Small Wings have a presentation for you. A poem, and then a play.

Fumiko guides him to a front-row seat in the audience, where she sits beside him.

Maiko dashes offstage. Akira nervously takes his place at centre stage.

AKIRA: Hana Brady, thirteen years old,
            Was the owner of this suitcase.
            Sixty-four years ago, May 18, 1942 —
            Two days after Hana's eleventh birthday —
            She was taken to Terezin in Czechoslovakia.
            October 23, 1944, crowded into the freight train,
            She was sent to Auschwitz.
            She was taken to the gas chamber right after.
            People were allowed to take only one suitcase with them.
            We wonder what Hana put in her suitcase.
            Hana would have been sixty-nine years old had she lived,
            But her life stopped when she was thirteen.
            We wonder what kind of girl she was.
            A few drawings she made at Terezin —
            These are the only things she left for us.
            What do these drawings tell us?
            Happy memories of her family?
            Dreams and hopes for the future?
            Why was she killed?
            There was one reason.
            She was born Jewish.
            Name: Hana Brady.
            Date of Birth: May 16, 1931.
            Orphan.
            We, Small Wings, will tell every child in Japan
            What happened to Hana.
            We, Small Wings, will never forget what happened to
            One-and-a-half-million Jewish children.
            We children can make a difference in building peace
            In the world —
            So that the Holocaust will never happen again.

Akira bows.

Lights dim. Akira takes his place behind Hana's suitcase.

Slowly, carefully, he unlocks the suitcase. He hesitates, then slowly opens the suitcase.

Maiko enters on a scooter and circles the stage.

Akira closes the suitcase. Maiko exits.

AKIRA: Hana!

Blackout.